Beyond Synthesis: Mastering VHDL for Efficient System Design

Nami

TABLE OF CONTENTS

CHAPTER 1: INTRODUCTION 1

   1.1   Book Outline 2

CHAPTER 2: VIRTUAL PROTOTYPING 5

   2.1   Rapid Application Specific Signal-processor Prototyping (RASSP) 5
   2.2   Benefits of Virtual Prototyping 6
   2.3   VHDL 7
      2.3.1   *The History of VHDL* 7
      2.3.2   *VHDL Standards* 7
      2.3.3   *VHDL Software* 7
   2.4   VHDL Coding 9
   2.5   VHDL Modelling 10
      2.5.1   *Temporal Resolution* 11
      2.5.2   *Data Resolution* 11
      2.5.3   *Functional Resolution* 11
      2.5.4   *Structural Resolution* 12
      2.5.5   *Software Programming Resolution* 12
   2.6   General Modelling Styles 12
      2.6.1   *Behavioural Model* 12
      2.6.2   *Functional Model* 12
      2.6.3   *Structural Model* 12
   2.7   System Models 13
      2.7.1   *Executable Specification* 13
      2.7.2   *Mathematical Model* 13
      2.7.3   *Algorithm Model* 13
   2.8   Location of Models 14

CHAPTER 3: FIELD PROGRAMMABLE GATE ARRAYS (FPGAS) 16

   3.1   What is an FPGA? 16
      3.1.1   *The Logic Cells* 17
      3.1.2   *The I/O Cells* 18
      3.1.3   *The Interconnect Matrix* 19
   3.2   Producing an FPGA Design 19
      3.2.1   *Design Entry* 19
      3.2.2   *Logic synthesis* 20
      3.2.3   *Place-and-route* 20
      3.2.4   *Programming the FPGA* 21
   3.3   Digital Signal Processing in FPGAs 21

CHAPTER 4: SYNTHETIC APERTURE RADAR..**24**

4.1   RADAR BASICS..24
4.2   SAR PROCESSING..26
    4.2.1   Overview..26
    4.2.2   Image Resolution...27

CHAPTER 5: PREPROCESSOR DESIGN **30**

5.1   OVERVIEW 30
5.2   CURRENT SYSTEM 31
5.3   PROPOSED SOLUTIONS 32
    5.3.1   Filtering with no Presummer 32
    5.3.2   Filtering after Presumming...32
5.4   FILTER DESIGN 33
5.5   PREPROCESSOR DEVELOPMENT..34
    5.5.1   Comparing the Proposed Solutions 35
    5.5.2   Finding the Optimal Filter..36
5.6   ALGORITHM MODEL..39

CHAPTER 6: HARDWARE DESIGN...**41**

6.1   HARDWARE REQUIREMENTS 41
6.2   MEMORY OVERVIEW 42
    6.2.1   Separate Memories..43
    6.2.2   Shared Memory 43
    6.2.3   Memory Organisation 44
    6.2.4   Memory Requirements 45
    6.2.5   Memory Selection..47
    6.2.6   VHDL Memory Model...47
6.3   HARDWARE EXPANDABILITY 48
    6.3.1   Multiple Output FIFOs 49
    6.3.2   Writeback to RAM 49
6.4   EXTERNAL INTERFACE...50

CHAPTER 7: PRESUMMER DESIGN..**51**

7.1   FUNCTIONAL MODEL...51
    7.1.1   Model Functionality 52
    7.1.2   Presummer Interface..52
    7.1.3   Model Overview 53
    7.1.4   State Machine 56
    7.1.5   Verification..57
7.2   FINAL IMPLEMENTATION..60
    7.2.1   State Machine Encoding 60
    7.2.2   DC Offset Removal..62
    7.2.3   Pipelining 63
    7.2.4   Component Instantiation...65
    7.2.5   Verification..66
    7.2.6   Target Device 68

CHAPTER 8: PREFILTER DESIGN **69**

8.1   THE FUNCTIONAL MODEL 69
    8.1.1   Model Functionality 69
    8.1.2   Prefilter Interface..70
    8.1.3   Model Overview 70
    8.1.4   State Machine...72
    8.1.5   Verification..73
8.2   FINAL IMPLEMENTATION..75
    8.2.1   State Machine...75
    8.2.2   FIR Filter...76

| | 8.2.3 | *Dividers* | *77* |

	8.2.3	*Dividers*	*77*
	8.2.4	*DC Offset*	*79*
	8.2.5	*Verification*	*80*
	8.2.6	*Target Device*	*81*

CHAPTER 9: CONCLUSIONS AND RECOMMENDATIONS **82**

APPENDIX A: FIR FILTER CHARACTERISTICS **84**

A.1	FILTER A	85
A.2	FILTER B	86
A.3	FILTER C	87
A.4	FILTER D	88
A.5	FILTER E	89
A.6	FILTER F	90
A.7	TABLE OF FILTER COEFFICIENTS	91

APPENDIX B: JTAG BOUNDARY SCAN **93**

APPENDIX C: MATHCAD SAR PROCESSOR **94**

APPENDIX D: VHDL CODE DESCRIPTION **100**

D.1	TEST DATA GENERATOR	100
D.2	RAM MODEL	100
D.3	PRESUMMER CODE	101
	D.3.1	*Algorithm Model*	*101*
	D.3.2	*Functional Model*	*102*
	D.3.3	*Synthesis Model*	*102*
	D.3.4	*Presummer Testbench*	*104*
D.4	PREFILTER CODE	104
	D.4.1	*Algorithm Model*	*104*
	D.4.2	*Functional Model*	*105*
	D.4.3	*Synthesis Model*	*106*
	D.4.4	*Prefilter Testbench*	*107*

REFERENCES **109**

Chapter 1: Introduction

VHDL is a hardware description language that is gaining increasing popularity with digital designers, as it is both a synthesis[1] and simulation language. The majority of users in South Africa today use only the language's synthesis abilities, hardly ever tapping into the power of simulation. Their systems design is modular and although their modules are tested, it is not known before the design is prototyped how the modules will function in the completed system. In South Africa, VHDL is used mostly for FPGA design. Most of the more popular FPGA design software packages have very limited VHDL simulation abilities. The system therefore cannot be tested before it is completely implemented.

With the fierce competition between companies to get their products onto the market, the design's time-to-market must be minimised. Finding design errors during physical prototyping leads to costly delays, both financial and timely. It would be far cheaper if the designs could be debugged and tested before reaching silicon for the first time. The solution is Virtual or System Level Prototyping.

Virtual Prototyping involves the simulation of the entire system. The level of complexity can be from a behavioural (top level), right down to a gate level simulation. The lack of use of Virtual Prototyping in smaller companies often is due to them not having sufficient resources to develop their own models of the components they wish to simulate. This is becoming less of a problem due to the rapidly increasing popularity of the World Wide Web. VHDL models can now be obtained for a variety of digital devices, from TTL and CMOS gates to models of processors that will execute given instruction code. Many specialist companies are publishing on the Web with their sole area of business being the development of such models. Companies are now able to purchase the models they require, rather than spending hundreds of man-hours developing them.

---

[1] Synthesis is the process of specifying digital logic gates that will be functionally equivalent to a specification of hardware described in a hardware description language.

This book will attempt to investigate the feasibility of VHDL simulation. As a case study, the design of a digital preprocessor for a synthetic aperture radar was attempted. The preprocessor was designed and simulated in VHDL.

The preprocessor was targeted for a Field Programmable Gate Array (FPGA). The reason for this was to investigate the level of complexity of algorithm that could be achieved in such a device. This solution was completely hardware based. A software based digital signal processor (DSP) solution is being investigated by Yann Tréméac [19].

1.1   Book Outline

This book is divided into 9 chapters and 4 appendices. A brief overview of each chapter and appendix follows:

Chapter 2 introduces Virtual Prototyping, which is part of a new design process called RASSP. <u>R</u>apid <u>A</u>pplication <u>S</u>pecific <u>S</u>ignal-processor <u>P</u>rototyping is a design methodology which aims to reduce the typical development time of a DSP system from months to a period of weeks. Virtual prototyping is also becoming a necessity owing to the increased pin counts of some of the new high density IC packages. It is no longer feasible for a "bed-of-nails" tester to test boards containing such devices and plugging a logic analyser into the system is almost impossible as the new packages often contain no pins e.g. Ball Grid Arrays. Virtual prototyping is required to test the internals of each of the PLDs while boundary scan techniques will test their interconnection. The chapter also introduces VHDL, a Hardware Description Language which can be used for both the simulation and synthesis of digital circuits. System components can be modelled with VHDL and chapter 2 describes the different levels of abstraction of these models. How each is used in the virtual prototyping process is also described.

Chapter 3 describes Field Programmable Gate Arrays and the design process required to produce the configuration files for programming them. Most FPGA manufacturers have design software for their specific devices. These packages will often compile a VHDL description of the device and then synthesise the logic required to implement it. This logic is then place-and-routed and a configuration file for the FPGA is produced. Many of the new FPGAs are SRAM based and required a specialised serial ROM to load their configuration on power up. The use of FPGAs in a DSP environment is also discussed.

Chapter 4 introduces some basic synthetic aperture radar theory. Since the focus of this book is not SAR processing, the theory contained in this chapter will not be very detailed. An overview of the workings of a pulsed radar will be described. Once the transmitted data has been received, it requires processing to convert it into a focussed image. In order to do this, the data has to be compressed in azimuth, so that the individual targets can be seen. Chapter 4 describes this process.

Chapter 5 details the filter development. This chapter begins by looking at why the preprocessor was needed and how its specifications were decided upon. At this stage of development, no consideration was given to the hardware. The preprocessor was required in an existing radar to reduce the data rate of the data being stored. By low pass filtering the data, it could safely be subsampled. Three main methods were examined: Using only a presummer, using a presummer before a FIR filter and using just a FIR filter. All of these methods were tested and the results are included. Using a presummer before the FIR filter was the method decided upon as it allowed for the use of a filter with a better cutoff. This produced a better focussed image.

Chapter 6 discusses the preprocessor's hardware development. A top down approach was used during development to keep in line with the principles of RASSP. Without specifying the internals of either the presummer or prefilter, some decisions had to be made regarding the hardware requirements, especially for the memory. The expandability of the solution had to be determined as the processing speed of the presummer and prefilter would not be known until it was designed. A solution which could be made to meet the speed requirements had to be found.

Chapters 7 and 8 describe the design of the presummer and prefilter FPGAs. A top level, behavioural simulation was first performed to verify the correctness of the algorithms. Once this was verified, separate high level models of the presummer and prefilter were constructed. This allowed the interaction of the components to be tested and the system could then be compared with the original algorithm. The presummer and prefilter were then implemented separately as synthesisable VHDL models. Once implemented, the components were then tested against the results produced by the original algorithmic simulation. The final design could therefore be verified without the need for physical prototyping.

Chapter 9 contains the conclusions. Virtual Prototyping has distinct advantages when building systems, whether it be simple micro-controller boards to complete digital radars. The ability to simulate each of the devices and to be able to probe any point in the system saves a great deal of time when debugging systems. Finding errors is far quicker when looking at the results of a simulation than having to use conventional hardware techniques such as logic analysers. Correcting errors is also far cheaper when discovered before the printed circuit boards are made. Depending on the simulator used, the number of existing VHDL models available to the designer varies. Producing models is a time consuming task and it would be pointless for small companies to employ a designer to code only the models required.

Appendix A contains the specifications for the different filters considered. The specifications include the tap weights, sampling frequency and cut-off frequency.

Appendix B contains brief description of the JTAG standard for programming FPGAs and for use in Boundary Scan.

Appendix C contains the MathCAD simulation used for comparing the effects of the filters on the SAR processing.

Appendix D contains the VHDL source code for the simulations and synthesised FPGA.

Chapter 2: Virtual Prototyping

Virtual prototyping is known by a variety of names including board level simulation, system simulation and rapid prototyping. Virtual prototyping can be defined as "simulating the functionality of one or several printed circuit boards built with standard components, possibly incorporating Application Specific Integrated Circuits, ASIC, and Application Specific Standard Products, ASSP" [8]

2.1   Rapid Application Specific Signal-processor Prototyping (RASSP)

Virtual prototyping is the basis for Rapid Application Specific Signal-processor Prototyping (RASSP). This program was initiated by the Defence Advanced Research Projects Agency (DARPA) in July 1993 with the aims of significantly improving the process by which embedded digital signal processors are developed and supported [17]. The program also emphasises design reuse in an effort to further reduce the development time of subsequent projects or upgrades. RASSP aims at reducing the time taken to field a prototype by a factor of four with respect to conventional design methodologies. One of the main reasons behind this program was that systems were designed using state-of-the-art devices, but by the time the system went into production, the devices were obsolete [15].

The RASSP methodology is based on two principal ideas: Concurrent design and design reuse [13]. The former specifies the idea that software and hardware should be developed in parallel and not serially, as is often the case. The hardware should also be developed in parallel with separate teams designing different modules of the design. Design reuse is also critical to this program as it is pointless repeating work which has already been done.

To test the claims of the RASSP program, a series of benchmarks were established. The first two required the development of a virtual prototype and a hardware prototype respectively for a Synthetic Aperture Radar Processor.

2.2   Benefits of Virtual Prototyping

Virtual prototyping encourages a top-down design methodology. This allows the entire system to be modelled at first on a very abstract level where the basic workings of the system can be verified. Once it is determined that the system will meet the processing requirements i.e. the algorithm to be implemented is correct, more specific and detailed models can be developed to replace the abstract ones. During this process, the system can be divided into modules and the specifications of each can be defined. By doing this at an early stage, the functionality of the modules can be tested, as well as their ability to interact with the other modules. By moving to lower levels of model abstraction, different architectures can be evaluated before one is finally chosen.

Virtual prototyping also allows for the simulation of subsystems which have not been fully implemented. This allows designers to test their individual modules with the modelled system, even if the entire system has not been implemented. Doing this enables the verification of each model within the system environment. As more modules are implemented, so their models are updated with more accurate ones (lower abstraction level).

Hardware and software partitioning has also been improved with the use of virtual prototyping. Under "traditional" development, once the hardware had been prototyped, the software could be developed.

Virtual prototyping allows a more thorough verification of the hardware than would be achieved using conventional hardware testing methods. One of the reasons for this is that virtual prototypes can be probed in many more places than conventional test hardware. Using these models will also allow the test engineer to test for conditions that are difficult to produce in the real hardware.

2.3   VHDL

<u>V</u>ery High Speed Integrated Circuit <u>H</u>ardware <u>D</u>escription <u>L</u>anguage is a hardware description language (HDL) which is rapidly gaining popularity as both a simulation and synthesis language.

2.3.1   The History of VHDL

In 1980 the US Department of Defence (DoD) funded a project under the Very High Speed Integrated Circuit (VHSIC) project to create a standard Hardware Description Language (HDL). The reason for this was the DoD's desire to obtain a standard design and documentation tool. The result of this was the creation of the VHSIC HDL, or VHDL as it is now commonly referred to [11].

2.3.2   VHDL Standards

VHDL is an IEEE standard and had undergone one revision. VHDL was standardised in 1987 by the IEEE and was referred to as VHDL 1076-87. It was revised in 1993 (VHDL '93) and most VHDL software packages use this version today. There are not many significant differences between the two versions except for file I/O. Under VHDL '87 there was no way to explicitly open and close a file. This has been remedied in VHDL '93.

Synopsys, a company who are the industry leaders in ASIC design software including VHDL compilers and synthesisers, have written some VHDL libraries which have now become fairly standard and are packaged with most VHDL simulators. These additions deal mostly with the file I/O of formatted text.

2.3.3   VHDL Software

Once compiled, VHDL source files can be synthesised or simulated. These two processes are very different and often not both fully supported in some software packages.

VHDL synthesis involves taking a VHDL source file and synthesising the digital logic that the source file describes. Not all synthesisers are created equal and one of the characteristics which separates the good from the bad synthesisers is their ability to optimise the logic they have created. Thus, the logic that they produce will be less efficient than from a good compiler in speed and/or area. Many FPGA manufacturers provide VHDL synthesisers with their FPGA design software but licences for these often have to be purchased separately.

A full simulator should be either VHDL '87 or VHDL '93 compliant. VHDL simulators are sometimes packaged with synthesisers but often in a stripped down version. These simulators are normally graphical simulators where the inputs have to be entered graphically – not written as a VHDL input file. This is very limiting in that writing a VHDL description for a given waveform is far easier than entering it graphically, especially when it is repetitive. These simulators usually do not have any support for file I/O and so test benches cannot be written to verify any data produced.

A number of different vendors produce VHDL Simulators. Some of these have demonstration versions of their software which may be evaluated for a short period. All except Ptolomy and Alliance are commercial packages.

- ActiveVHDL

- Alliance. This is a freeware VHDL teaching aid which supports some of the VHDL subset.

- Mentor Graphics

- Model Technology's ModelSim

- PeakVHDL

- Ptolemy. This is written by the Ptolemy Project at the University of California at Berkeley.

- Synopsys

2.4   VHDL Coding

Describing the VHDL language is far too great a task to perform here. What follows is a brief introduction into the structure of the language. The main programming unit in VHDL source is the entity-architecture pair (see Figure 1). An *entity* is the description of the interface ports of a design e.g. the pins on an IC. This entity has an *architecture* associated with it that describes the working of the entity. If an entity is required as part of another entity, it is referred to as a component and is declared as such.

An entity can have multiple architectures associated with it, although only one architecture may be used at any one time. A *configuration* is required to bind an architecture with an entity (see Figure 1). If there is no explicit configuration, the default configuration is used.

VHDL source written for simulation cannot always be synthesised. In fact, only a small subset of the language is synthesisable. This alone is reason enough for having multiple architectures. For the same entity, synthesisable and simulatable architectures can be written. Depending on which process is being performed, either of the two architectures can be selected in the configuration (see Figure 1).

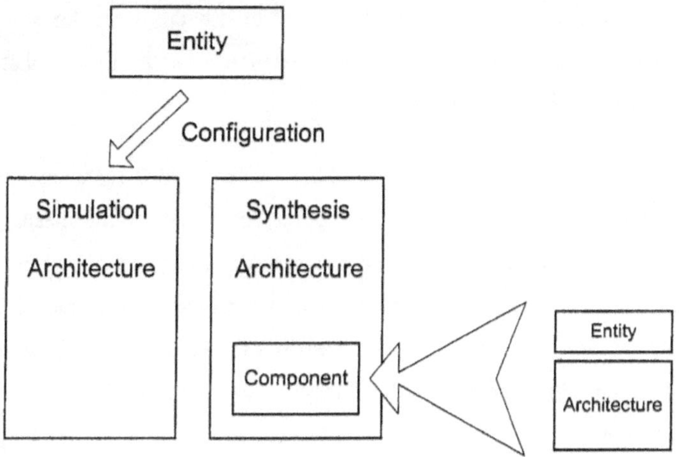

Figure 1: VHDL Entity Architecture Pairs

The style of writing VHDL will also affect the logic that is synthesised. Although two ways of writing some code will have the same logical effect, the logic synthesised could be completely different. For example, using a "case" statement is more efficient than using nested "if" statements. The former is often synthesised as a multiplexer while the latter results in a string of nested AND gates.

Writing synthesisable VHDL cannot be compared with writing a program in another software programming language like "C" or even simulation VHDL. One must always remember that one is writing hardware and that the source which is written is going to be transformed into hardware. Writing code without considering the hardware that will be generated will result in code with either does not synthesise or does not perform as expected. An example of this causes latches to be inferred if signals are not assigned default values.

2.5   VHDL Modelling

A VHDL model of a device is a description written in VHDL which describes the operation of the device at a particular level of abstraction. To introduce standardisation into the writing of VHDL models, the RASSP Taxonomy Working Group (RTWG) was formed in 1995. Their mission was to "develop a systematic basis for defining VHDL model types and to use this basis for concisely and unambiguously defining a terminology that describes the models that are used within a RASSP design process" [14].

To describe a VHDL model, the RASSP Taxonomy differentiates between five orthogonal model characteristics: Temporal detail, data value detail, functional detail, structural detail and software programming level. Each of these characteristics is applied to the internal and external views of the model. These can be plotted on a set of axes [14] that describes the level of abstraction of each of these model characteristics. A brief explanation of these characteristics can be found below.

2.5.1 *Temporal Resolution*

The Temporal Resolution Axis represents the time scale of the events that are modelled [14]. For example if one is wishing to capture the timing of the gate delays, the temporal resolution of the model could be in the order of picoseconds. If, on the other hand, the instruction cycles were to be modelled, the temporal resolution of the model could be in the order of milliseconds.

2.5.2 *Data Resolution*

The Data Resolution Axis represents the resolution of the format of the data values that are used [14]. For example, if the value 1 was to be represented, it could be done so on a low level as a binary string "0001". The same number could be represented as an integer (1) or as an enumerated type e.g. Yellow. All these representations are equally accurate, just increasingly abstract.

2.5.3 *Functional Resolution*

The Functional Resolution Axis represents the level of detail at which the model describes the functionality of the component or system [14]. This can range from Boolean expressions that specify the logic required to implement a function to the mathematical representation of that function.

2.5.4   Structural Resolution

The Structural Resolution Axis represents the level of detail that a model provides about how it is constructed out of constituent parts [14]. For example, if the structure of an IC were being modelled, a high resolution model would describe the IC in terms of the logic gates which make it up. A low resolution model would describe an IC in terms of ALUs, multiplexers and registers.

2.5.5   Software Programming Resolution

The Software Programming Resolution Axis represents the granularity of the instructions a model can execute when running the target software [14]. The resolution can range from microcode instructions to high level operations like an FFT.

2.6   General Modelling Styles

For a complete discussion of VHDL modelling, the reader is urged to consult [14] as it provides a complete reference for all types of VHDL models, not only the ones introduced here. All VHDL models are described in terms of three primary classes. Each of these uses the axes described in Section 2.5 to describe their resolution.

2.6.1   Behavioural Model

This model describes the functionality and timing of a component without specifying a particular implementation. It can be thought of as a functional model with timing. A behavioural model can exist at any level of abstraction – this being determined by the resolution of the implementation details [14].

2.6.2   Functional Model

This model describes the function of the system without introducing timing. It is essentially a behavioural model without the timing. Like the behavioural model, the functional model can exist at any level of abstraction [14].

2.6.3   Structural Model

A structural model describes a component or system in terms of the interconnection of sub-components. The model shows the structure of the physical implementation.

For example, a structural model of a processor would show, among other things, an ALU connected with some registers and a program counter. These sub-components can be described behaviourally, functionally or structurally [14].

2.7   System Models

The RTWG defines three terms for use in describing models that represent digital systems. These models contain no structural information regarding the implementation of the system.

2.7.1   Executable Specification

This model is a behavioural description of the system or component and mirrors the particular functionality and timing of the required system or component. Other system metrics e.g. weight, power consumption and size can be included in this model [14].

2.7.2   Mathematical Model

The mathematical model describes the functional relationship between the input and output data values. This relationship described in purely mathematical terms but does not contain any indication as to which mathematical method is used in the computation. This description can be found in the algorithm model [14].

A mathematical model is written to test the mathematics behind the processing to verify that they are correct. Once this is verified, an algorithm model can be written to test various implementations of the mathematics.

2.7.3   Algorithm Model

This is similar to the mathematical model in that it too describes the relationship between the input and output data values. The difference is that the algorithm model also describes how the results are calculated i.e. using Newton's method or a McLauren Series [14].

An algorithm model is used to test the efficiency and validity of a number of chosen mathematical methods. This model is also used to test the required precision of data values.

2.8   Location of Models

There are a number of sources of VHDL models. Most of these are on the World Wide Web and the designer is able to download the model(s) he/she is looking for. Certain VHDL Simulator Manufacturers provide models for use with their software. Synopsys is one such company and probably have the largest selection of models. The following lists a number of web sites which contain either freeware or shareware models.

- **The RASSP Home Page** has a number of VHDL models. These include processor, memory and bus models and are available for free download.

- **The Free Model Foundation** provides some free and other commercial models.

- **The Hamburg VHDL Archive** provides freeware and shareware models.

- **The University of Strasbourg** has a free model archive.

- **The Microsystems Prototyping Laboratory at Mississippi State University** has some free VHDL models.

- **Doulos VHDL Model Library** have some free behavioural models.

A number of commercial model developers also have web sites. Since these models have to be paid for before they can be evaluated, the quality of these sites has yet to be determined.

Chapter 3: Field Programmable Gate Arrays (FPGAs)

Field Programmable Gate Arrays (FPGAs) are programmable logic devices which provide the benefits of custom CMOS VLSI, while avoiding the initial cost, long development cycle and inherent risk of a conventional masked gate array [20].

3.1   What is an FPGA?

When custom digital logic is required in a design, the designer is provided with a number of options ranging from ASICs to discrete logic. ASICs are expensive to design but their unit price is low since the size of the minimum order is usually very big. The designer specifies the logic required in the IC and the manufacturer produces it from a design file. An FPGA is a type of ASIC except that the designer can configure the logic within the device to implement the required functionality. The FPGA effectively provides the designer with a "sea of logic gates" which is configured by the designer. This process has the effect of connecting the logic gates in such a way that the required logic functions are produced. The unit price of an FPGA is more than an ASIC but FPGAs are available in smaller quantities. The initial cost of production is less for an FPGA than an ASIC since the internals of the former are already specified. All that is required is for the device to be configured to produce the required functionality. When designing an ASIC, the entire design of the device is left to the designer. More skill is therefore required to design an ASIC than to produce an FPGA. FPGAs are often used as prototypes for ASICs. The FPGAs can be programmed to provide the same functionality as the ASICs for testing purposes.

Different manufacturers have different structures for their devices but essentially they share the same basic idea[2]. There are three parts: the logic cells, the I/O cells and the interconnection matrix. These are illustrated in Figure 2.

Many FPGAs are SRAM based and read their configuration from an onboard ROM on power up. This has a number of advantages:

- Bug fixes can be performed by simply reprogramming the configuration ROM.

- The FPGA can be forced to reconfigure "in system" to allow it to perform different tasks as required [10] e.g. if the FPGA contained a FIR filter, new coefficients could be loaded if required. These configurations would have to be stored onboard and could not be created "on the fly".

- For applications where the security of the internal design is critical, the contents of both the ROM and the FPGA can be erased should the unit be tampered with. Once erased, no reverse engineering can take place as no clue as to the operations of the device will remain.

3.1.1   The Logic Cells

The logic cells are blocks of logic that can be configured to produce the user's required logic functionality. These logic cells contain flip-flops and some logic function generators which are usually implemented as lookup tables.

The LUTs have a set number of inputs but still provide incredible flexibility since logic cells can be combined with the interconnect matrix. This allows multiple LUTs to be used to generate a single function.

In some FPGAs, RAM and ROM are available to the designer. These memory devices are sometimes implemented in the LUTs in the logic cells (e.g. Xilinx), while other devices have separate cells to implement them (e.g. Altera).

---

[2] The description below is essentially what the two market leaders in FPGA technology, Xilinx Inc. and Altera Corp. use.

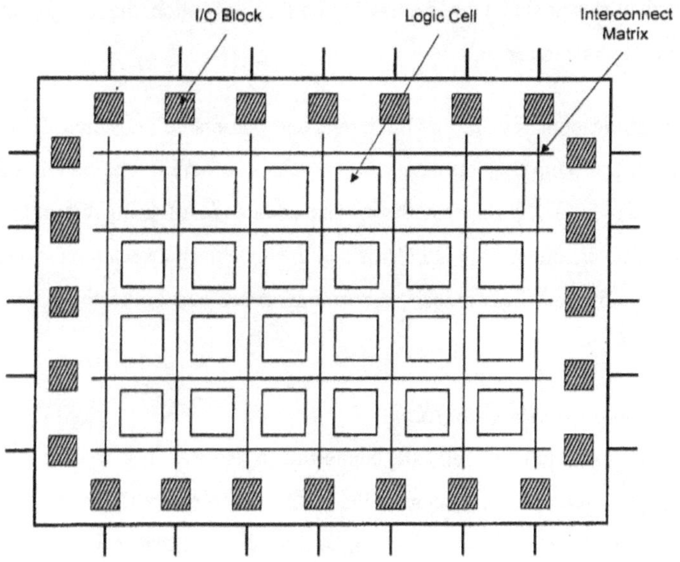

Figure 2: FPGA Internals

FPGAs are rich in registers as each logic cell contains a number of flip-flops. This makes them ideal for pipelined designs.

Some devices contain carry logic that allows a carry signal to be included in a logic cell. This can reduce the number of logic cells used for complex functions in that without carry chains, extra logic cells would be required to implement these functions.

3.1.2   The I/O Cells

I/O cells are similar to the logic cells except the logic that they contain is more specifically tailored to I/O functions. These cells provide the interface between the external device package pins and the internal logic. Each I/O cell is associated with an external package pin and can be configured for input, output or bi-directional signals.

Sometimes the I/O cells offer programmable slew rates. The slew rate of an output is a measure of the speed at which it can change. Faster slew rates produce more noise than slower slew rates. Depending on the application, the designer can choose which slew rate to use.

Many applications require that the inputs and outputs be registered. In an effort to minimise the setup time on inputs and the clock to output time on outputs, the I/O cells often have flip-flops in them. The advantage of using these flip-flops as opposed to any others in the FPGA is that the distance between the pin and the flip-flop is minimised. This reduces the routing delay and hence the setup and hold times of the pin.

3.1.3 The Interconnect Matrix

The logic cells and I/O cells are connected together with a routing matrix. This matrix provides a means of connecting cells to each other. Different vendors have different methods of providing routing and most claim that their devices are more "routable" than their competitors, especially when referring to pin locking. Pin locking is when the designer forces the FPGA design software to place certain input and output signals on specified pins. When the FPGA is initially designed, these signals are placed on the pins that are most optimal in terms of routing. Should the design be changed after the PCB had been designed, it is essential that the FPGA use the original pins for its signals. Obviously, this problem increases as the utilisation of the FPGA increases.

3.2 Producing an FPGA Design

FPGA vendors produce software that is used in design of their own devices. The device specific stage of the design is the fitting or place-and-routing. Third party software is available to perform the design entry and logic synthesis but the author has not encountered any which can perform any device fitting.

3.2.1 Design Entry

This is the first stage in the design. Two methods exist for doing this: graphical or HDL entry. Graphical entry is cumbersome with larger designs and is less flexible than HDL entry. Symbols for various logic functions (logic gates, multiplexers, adders etc.) are connected together by the designer. This method is useful if a schematic for the required logic already exists but becomes very cluttered with larger designs.

HDL entry is not limited to using VHDL. ABEL, AHDL and Verilog are examples of other hardware description languages that can be used for describing the operation of the device. Different design software supports different HDLs but most seem to offer VHDL support – usually as an optional extra.

Once the design has been entered, it has to be compiled. This checks the syntax of the source (if HDL entry is used) and converts it onto an intermediate format which is more useful to a computer. This compiled source is passed to the logic synthesiser.

3.2.2   Logic synthesis

The logic synthesiser takes the compiled source and produces a digital logic equivalent for it. The logic produced is optimised for the device that is targeted. Design software has device specific libraries that contain information on the available logic in different devices.

Most synthesisers can be controlled in the optimisation of the synthesised logic. The trade off between logic speed and area or routability can be set by the designer. The use of carry chains (see section 3.1.1) can also be enabled.

3.2.3   Place-and-route

Once the logic has been synthesised, the fitting software has to perform a place-and-route. This process takes all the synthesised logic and connects it inside the FPGA. All the I/O pins are also connected to the corresponding I/O cells and these in turn are connected to the required logic cells. This is a complex process and often takes the largest proportion of the compile time.

If the fitter cannot perform the place-and-route on the targeted device, it will either, at the designer's request, split the design into multiple devices or use a larger capacity device.

3.2.4   *Programming the FPGA*

Once the place-and-route has taken place, a configuration file is generated for the target device. Since most FPGAs currently used are SRAM based, they have to be programmed or configured on power up. There are a number of ways of performing this but the most common is to use a serial programming ROM. This ROM has an internal address counter and it provides the required signals and data to the FPGA to program it. FPGAs are often programmed via their JTAG port. More information on JTAG can be found in Appendix B: JTAG Boundary Scan.

3.3   Digital Signal Processing in FPGAs

The choice to use a DSP chip or an FPGA is not always an easy one. Both DSPs and FPGAs have increased in speed and are continuing to do so. DSPs are available off the shelf and anyone who is proficient in the C programming language should be able to program most of them. FPGAs can be designed graphically so a designer who is unfamiliar with VHDL can still produce and FPGA.

The main difference between an FPGA and DSP is that a DSP is a general purpose processor while an FPGA can be used to implement an architecture that is optimised to perform one specific task. This is not to say that the FPGA cannot be reprogrammed to perform another task but rather the architecture that the DSP program makes use of is fixed. That DSP architecture is a general architecture that is designed to support a number of different functions. The functionality of the FPGA is programmed by the designer to be optimal for the task being performed.

With the introduction of SRAM based FPGAs, reprogramming either type of device with updated code is a trivial task and can often be done "in circuit". Compile times for larger designs will be longer for the FPGAs than the DSPs because the DSPs require no place-and-routing. On more complicated designs however, modifying the operation of a DSP is simpler than performing the same operation on an FPGA. The DSP modification can require the addition of just a few lines of code while the FPGA equivalent of that code could require the addition of a large amount of logic.

Optimising the design to meet the required speed can be more tricky in an FPGA than with a DSP. With the DSP, the instruction time of each operation is fixed and the more code that has to be processed, the longer it will take. If the code cannot be simplified any further then either more devices need to be added in improve the processing power or a faster device needs to be used.

With an FPGA, the same is true to an extent: The more complex the function, the more logic is required and the longer the result will take. The difference with the FPGA is that there are a number of other factors that influence the operating speed. Firstly there is the speed of the device – FPGAs are available in different speed grades. The same logic on a faster device will obviously result in faster operation. Secondly, there is the efficiency of the synthesiser. A poor synthesiser will not optimise the logic to the same extent as a higher quality one. The result will be slower logic. Thirdly, the tasks that are to be performed can possibly be run in parallel, often to a larger extent than multiprocessor DSPs. Lastly there is pipelining. A highly pipelined system will have a larger data throughput than one which isn't. Although DSP architectures often include data and instruction pipelining, the pipeline is often not as long as a custom designed FPGA. It is often a challenge to make an FPGA work at a high speed. In a DSP system, the multiplication is a fixed operation; there is one instruction to perform it. In an FPGA, multiplication can be performed in a number of ways e.g. Partial Product LUT Multipliers, Constant Coefficient Multipliers and Scaling Accumulator Multipliers [5].

Ultimately the choice between the two processors has to be made after considering the algorithm. Multiplication in FPGAs is costly in terms of logic and the speed of DSP multipliers is often faster than those synthesised in FPGAs. On the other hand, if the multiplication is small i.e. the widths of the multiplier and multiplicand are small, a LUT based implementation could be used which and can be performed in a single clock cycle.

An area where DSPs excel compared to FPGAs is in the support of floating point operations. Most of the DSP functions which have been written for FPGAs are only capable of performing integer operations. DSPs, on the other hand, are available in both fixed and floating point versions. If the required processing makes use of floating point operations, a DSP is the clear choice.

Chapter 4:   Synthetic Aperture Radar

Synthetic Aperture Radar (SAR) is an imaging technique which is used for creating radar backscatter maps of the ground surface below a moving platform. This platform is usually either airborne or spaceborne. The treatment of the data from both platforms is fairly similar - the airborne case is examined here for short pulse operation.

4.1   Radar Basics

A radar transmits an electromagnetic pulse and times how long it takes for a reflection from a target to return. The further away the target is from the radar, the longer the delay between the transmitted and received pulses. If the target is moving radially relative to the radar when the transmitted pulse hits, a phase shift (Doppler Shift) will be introduced in the reflection. By observing the change in phase of the reflected signal, the radial speed of the target can be calculated.

SAR makes use of a coherent pulsed radar which describes a radar that transmits and receives alternately. After a short pulse has been transmitted, the radar switches to receive mode to receive the reflected returns from the target. Pulses are transmitted to provide regularly spaced samples along the flight track (azimuth direction). The time interval between pulses is known as the Pulse Repetition Interval (PRI) and is the inverse of the Pulse Repetition Frequency (PRF). This is shown in Figure 3.

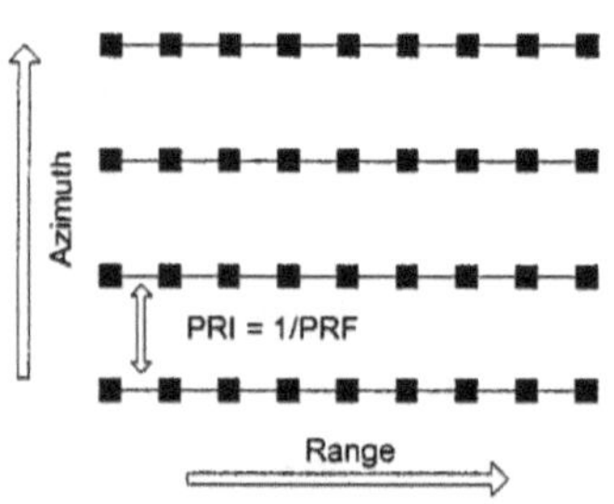

Figure 3: Radar Timing Relationships

Current radars are, for the most part, digital systems. When the radar begins receiving the reflections from its transmission, I Q demodulation is performed followed by an analogue to digital conversion. Complex sampling is used so that the phase information of the signal is not lost. For strip-mapping SAR, the sampling always starts a fixed time after the transmission ends. This is important as it allows each sample to represent a particular range bin. Each range bin has a corresponding ground resolution. Thus the returns from a stationary target (relative to the radar) will always appear in the same range bin.

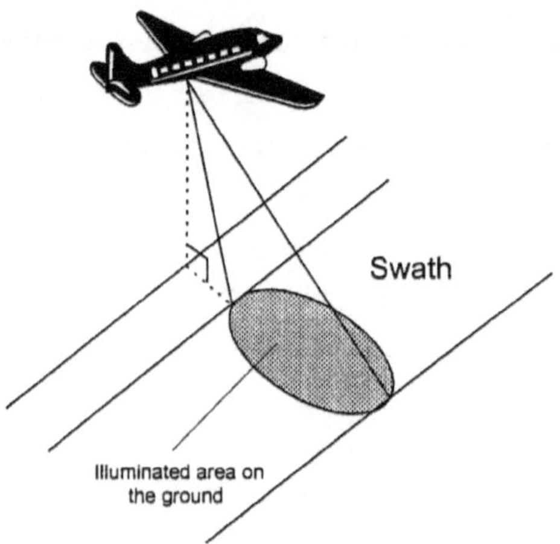

Figure 4: Illuminated Ground Area of a Side Looking Airborne Radar

With SAR, the radar antenna is usually mounted perpendicular to the flight path of the aircraft and is pointed downwards toward the ground. The antenna has a fixed beamwidth and so an oval shaped footprint is illuminated by the radar. In this way, as the aircraft flies along its flight path, the radar will illuminate a swath on the ground (see Figure 4). As the azimuth beamwidth is fairly large, a target is illuminated a number of times by successive transmission pulses as it travels through the beamwidth of the antenna. If the target is stationary on the ground, as the aircraft flies past it, the distance to the target will change. If the distance to the target were plotted, it would be hyperbolic as shown in the top block of Figure 5. This is known as range migration.

4.2   SAR Processing

4.2.1   Overview

Since the target is illuminated multiple times, the resulting image needs to be "focussed" so that the exact position of the target can be identified. Convolving with a matched filter for the target achieves this. The matched filter is constructed by simulating the return from a single point target and taking the time reversed, complex conjugate of it. The filter is applied in azimuth (the direction of flight of the aircraft).

The matched filter is then convolved with the returned data. Once the matched filter has been applied, the image is said to be focussed. The position of individual targets in azimuth can now be identified by locating peaks in the focussed data. A block diagram of the processing can be seen in Figure 5.

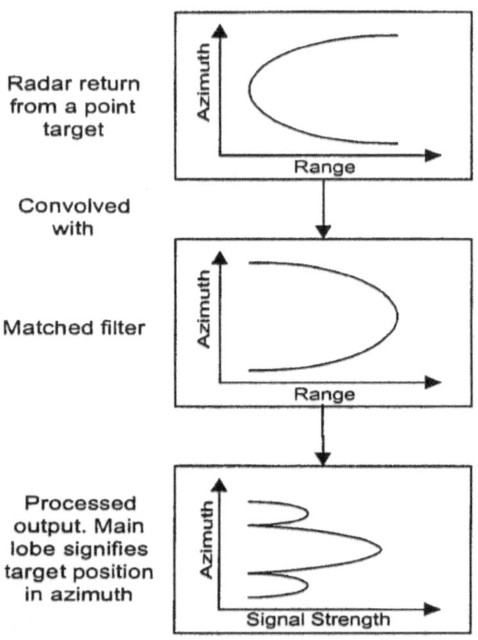

Figure 5: Block Diagram of SAR Processing

4.2.2   Image Resolution

For the ideal case, the azimuth resolution of a SAR is determined by the platform speed (the aircraft speed if it is aircraft mounted) and azimuth bandwidth of the system (see Equation 1). The value of K is determined by the type on windowing function that is used (0.89 is used for rectangular windows) [9]. This azimuth bandwidth is not to be confused with the azimuth sampling rate (PRF) but rather it is the Doppler bandwidth shown in Equation 2. In that equation, v is the platform speed, θ is the antenna azimuth beamwidth and λ is the carrier wavelength.

$$\mathrm{Re}s_{Azimuth} = K\frac{v}{Bandwidth_{Azimuth}}$$ Equation 1

$$Bandwidth_{Azimuth} = \frac{4v\sin(\frac{\theta}{2})}{\lambda}$$ Equation 2

Once the image has been focussed as described above, the power output of the focussed returns around the area of the target appear similar to a $\frac{\sin(x)}{x}$ function, as seen in the bottom block of Figure 5. This $\frac{\sin(x)}{x}$ function is formed as the result of the inverse Fourier Transform of a Rect function since the frequency spectrum of the transmitted wave, the received wave and the matched filter are all approximately Rect functions.

Three measures often used with point targets to determine the quality of the focussed image are: The width of the main peak, the peak sidelobe level and the integrated sidelobe level. The width of the peak, taken at the –3dB points, is used to calculate the actual azimuth resolution of the radar. The azimuth resolution is calculated by multiplying the peak width (measured in number of samples) by the sample size given by $\frac{v}{PRF}$ which is the ground spacing of the samples. During the convolution process, sidelobes are introduced into the output. These sidelobes appear as ghost targets in the focussed image, regularly spaced from the main target. The brightness of these ghost targets is related to the sidelobe level. It is therefore necessary to minimise the sidelobes to prevent the introduction of ghost images in the focussed image. A method of reducing them is to apply a window function to the matched filter. This has the effect of widening the main peak but also further reducing the sidelobes. Using a Hamming window will reduce the peak sidelobe level to approximately –40dB, compared to a rectangular window which provides sidelobe levels of approximately –13dB. A Hamming window will have a window factor of 1.30 in Equation 1 [9].

The integrated sidelobe level gives a measure of how much of the radar energy returns are in the sidelobes compared to the amount in the target return peak.

The resolution of a SAR in both range and azimuth is bandwidth limited. The theoretical maximum azimuth resolution is given in Equation 1 while the theoretical maximum range resolution is given in Equation 3. Note that there is also a window factor incorporated here for the window function that is used in range compression.

A measure the effectiveness of the SAR processing and the quality of the radar can be made by comparing the theoretical resolution of the radar with its measured performance.

$$Re\,solution_{Range} = K_{range}\,\frac{c}{2\,Bandwidth_{Tx\_pulse}}$$

Equation 3

Chapter 5: Preprocessor Design

5.1   Overview

This preprocessor was designed for the airborne SASAR 1 VHF (141MHz) Radar, set to undergo flight testing in mid 1998. As the name implies, the SASAR Radar was the South African Synthetic Aperture Radar. The radar sampled the return from its transmission with a pair of analogue to digital converters. Before this digital data could be stored, it had to be processed as the current data recorders could not record at the required data rate when the radar sampled at 4096 range bins per PRI.

The processing requirements were therefore to reduce the data rate of the sampled data, thus allowing the data recorders to store all the data. This processing was not to contaminate the data in any way which could negatively affect any SAR processing which would be performed at a later stage. This meant that the processing could not introduce any phase shift into the data. It would however be advantageous if the processing could improve the signal to noise ratio of the data.

The following table lists some of the important radar specifications:

Table 1: Radar Specifications

Pulse Repetition Frequency	625Hz
Carrier Frequency	141MHz
Pulse Width	88ns
Max Range Resolution	13.2m
Azimuth Beamwidth	45°
Elevation Beamwidth	60°
Aircraft Ground Speed	250m/sec
Range samples per PRI (I,Q)	2048/4096
Maximum Doppler Bandwidth	180Hz

To lower the data rate, the effective pulse repetition frequency had to be reduced since reducing the number of range samples per PRI would have reduced the performance of the radar. When processing SAR images, it is often desirable to make the azimuth and range resolution of the focussed image the same. The range resolution of the SASAR system was approximately 13 meters. SAR processing required that the azimuth bandwidth was approximately 37Hz to be able to focus the image to approximately 13 meters in azimuth with 2 independent looks for speckle reduction. Thus, the full 180Hz bandwidth which was available (see Table 1) was not required. The radar was sampling at a rate of 625Hz in azimuth. By reducing the azimuth sampling rate (PRF), the data rate would be reduced. The PRF could be reduced by a factor of 12 to give an effective PRF of 52Hz, slightly above the required 37Hz processing bandwidth. Since complex sampling was used, the Nyquist Sampling Rate was 37Hz.

The simplest method of reducing the azimuth sampling rate was to only store every n^{th} range line. Other methods existed which did not discard valuable data or result in aliasing and these made use of a low pass filter. By low pass filtering the data, the higher frequency components were removed. The signal could then safely be subsampled without infringing the Nyquist Sampling Criterion.

5.2   Current System

The current system made use of a presummer. The process of presumming involved calculating the average of a number of PRIs, thus implementing a crude low pass filter. Consecutive range lines were added to produce a single range line output. This adding took place in azimuth i.e. the corresponding range bins in each PRI were added. If a presummer of factor five were used then five range lines would be added to give one range line output. Presumming the data would have increased the signal to noise ratio as the noncoherent noise would have been added together and cancelled itself while the coherent signal would not.

Before considering alternative solutions, modifications to the current system were considered. The only possible modification was to increase the presum factor to the required value of 12. This would have reduced the data rate and increased the signal to noise ratio as a number of PRIs would be summed to give the filter output. The noncoherent noise would therefore sum to zero and only the signal would remain. The problem with method was that the Nyquist Sampling Criterion was infringed by doing this as the data contained frequency components of 180Hz, as given by the Maximum Doppler Bandwidth in Table 1. For this reason, other solutions had to be investigated.

5.3 Proposed Solutions

Two methods of filtering were examined. The first involved a low pass filter with a sampling frequency of 625Hz and a bandwidth of 20Hz while the second method was a combination of a presummer and a filter. Both these methods were tested as described in Section 5.5.1.

5.3.1 Filtering with no Presummer

This method required that a low pass filter be applied to the data in the azimuth direction. The low pass filtering would null the frequency components which were higher than approximately 20Hz [3]. This would constrain the bandwidth of the signal to approximately 40Hz so the data could safely be subsampled at 52Hz. The signal to noise ratio would be increased since the returns from many PRIs would be combined to form a single output.

5.3.2 Filtering after Presumming

A combination the current system design and the method described above was also possible. In this method, a presummer would be used to reduce the PRF to a value just higher than the Doppler Bandwidth of the system. This would be achieved by presumming the data by a factor of three and would reduce the effective PRF to 208.33Hz. A presum factor of three was the largest that could be used without infringing the Nyquist Sampling Criterion since the bandwidth of the signal was 180Hz. A low pass filter could then be used to remove the high frequency components of the signal before it was subsampled at 52Hz. The advantage of this

---

[3] The filter is obviously not a brick wall filter and so some higher frequency components will be passed. The attenuation in the stop band is finite so the higher frequencies will still be present although at a greatly reduced level.

method was that a filter with a steeper cutoff could be achieved with a fewer number of taps.

5.4   Filter Design

Digital filters were available in two flavours: Finite Impulse Response (FIR) and Infinite Impulse Response (IIR). The former was the easier of the two to implement as it simply consisted of a tapped delay line where each tap is multiplied by a scaling factor. More importantly, the filter required a linear phase response so that it did not adversely affect the SAR processing of the data - a process that relied on accurate phase measurements. Symmetric FIR filters with real coefficients have this characteristic [12].

The design of a FIR filter was centred around the sampling frequency of the data it operated on. Operating the same filter on data with different sampling rates produced different filter characteristics.

FIR filters are defined by a number of characteristics including the number of filter taps, their corresponding coefficients and the amount of ripple in the passband. The relationship between the filter coefficients and the frequency response of the filter can be seen in Equation 4 [12], where H_d is the ideal frequency response of the filter and n is the sample number. This implies that an infinite length filter is required to accurately describe the frequency response of a filter. The number of taps used affects the accuracy of the frequency response of the filter; the longer the filter, the more accurate the representation.

$$h_d[n] = \frac{1}{2\pi} \int_{-\pi}^{\pi} H_d(e^{j\omega})e^{j\omega n}\,dn \qquad\qquad \text{Equation 4}$$

There are a number of methods for calculating the filter coefficients and these are usually performed by computer. Two filter design packages were used: Matlab and QED (a part of the COSSAP package written by Synopsys). Matlab source code was provided in [16]. The design of filters is beyond the scope of this document but it is sufficient to mention that there are two main methods for calculating the filter coefficients: a window method and an optimal approximation method. Both of these methods were used in the design of a number of filters.

The FIR filter was required to perform a low pass filter to limit the bandwidth of the data to 40Hz. Once it was known that the data contained no frequency components higher than 20Hz, it could safely be subsampled at 52Hz since the bandwidth of the signal was 40Hz. The integrity of the data would remain intact. This subsampling could have been achieved in two ways. Firstly, every n^{th} processed sample could have been output while the rest were discarded. The problem with this method was that the available data was not being fully utilised, which was inefficient. Secondly, the FIR filter could have had a "skip factor" incorporated in it. The FIR filter would calculate a single output and then skip a number of samples before outputting another sample. An example of this is shown for a FIR filter with seven taps and a skip factor of four in Figure 6.

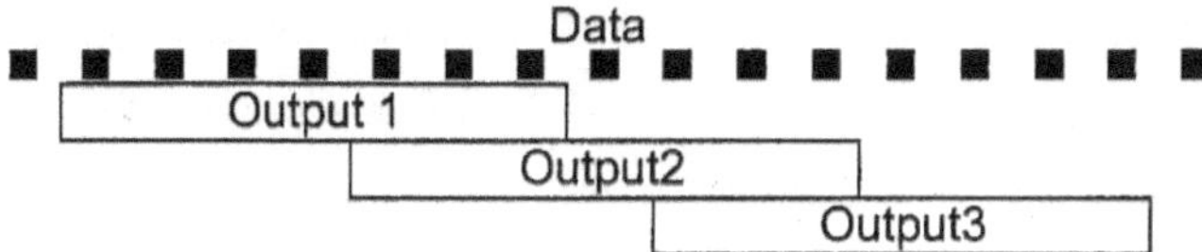

Figure 6: FIR Filter Skip Factor

5.5 Preprocessor Development

The two methods that were proposed in Section 5.3 were tested to determine the most suitable approach. Once a method was chosen, it was optimised. A number of methods existed for designing FIR Filters. To compare the results of the two proposed solutions, the same filter design method was used to produce filters that were identical except for the number of taps and sampling frequency. Details of the filters can be found in Appendix A: FIR Filter Characteristics.

Filter design is sometimes approached as more art than science as the responses of the different filters are often compared visually. Some produce better cutoffs while others have less ripple. For this reason it was decided to generate the filters and test their effects on the SAR processing. This produced more quantitative result of the quality of the FIR filter. A MathCAD SAR processor was written (see Appendix C: MathCAD SAR Processor) to generate synthetic SAR data of a point target. This data was then filtered and processed.

A peak detection program written by Jasper Horrell provided the numerical results. The input data to this program was the power values of the focussed SAR data. The program searched through the data to find the maximum value which signified the main peak. The gradient of the data was then examined to find the turning points on either side of the maximum value. The distance between these turning points was defined as the main peak width. The peak sidelobe level was found by searching through the data which did not fall into the main peak region and finding the maximum. The integrated sidelobe level was also calculated by integrating the main lobe and then integrating the sidelobes. The integrated sidelobe level was calculated as follows: *Integrated Sidelobe Level* $\equiv \frac{Integrated\ Sidelobes}{Integrated\ Main\ Lobe}$. Since there were an infinite number of sidelobes, a region of 200 samples around the main peak was used in the sidelobe calculations. The number of samples chosen was arbitrary but was constant for all calculations. These measurements provided a quantitative evaluation of the effects of the filter.

5.5.1 Comparing the Proposed Solutions

The number of filter taps was unknown and so it was decided to test 2 arbitrary filter lengths, 64 and 32 taps. The results of this gave an indication as to the required number of filter taps. Filter A (see Section A.1) was a 64 tap filter with a sampling frequency of 625Hz. A 32 tap filter, with the same specifications, was attempted but could not be produced since the number of taps was too small for the required response. Filter A was tested and the results can be seen in Table 2.

Filter B was constructed to be the same as Filter A except that its sampling frequency was 208 Hz. This filter operated on data which had been presummed by a factor of three. Filter B was then shortened to 32 taps (Filter C) and the test repeated. The results can be seen in Table 2.

The expected results were obtained. Filter A performed the worst as the azimuth resolution obtained was less than half of the filters. The reason for this can be attributed to the very wide passband, as can be seen in Figure 29. This introduced aliasing as the filter cutoff frequency was higher than the new sampling frequency of 52 Hz. It was expected that the longer filter would produce better results. This was partly true in that the longer filter produced a finer azimuth resolution. What was interesting was that the shorter filter (Filter C) had lower sidelobes than Filter B. The reason for this is unclear and is an area that requires further investigation. The difference between filters B and C was negligible in terms of resolution. Since an azimuth resolution of six meters was required, it was decided to use a 32 tap filter as that would ease processing requirements.

Table 2: Initial Test Filter Performance

Name	No. of Taps	Sampling Frequency	Azimuth Resolution	Peak Sidelobe Level	Integrated Sidelobe Level
Filter A	64	625 Hz	11.064 m	-12.619 dB	-18.411 dB
Filter B	64	208 Hz	5.268 m	-13.749 dB	-11.513 dB
Filter C	32	208 Hz	5.352 m	-14.840 dB	-13.347 dB

5.5.2 *Finding the Optimal Filter*

The solution to be implemented had been decided upon and was then optimised. A number of different filters were calculated and tested to find one which provided the optimal effects on the SAR processing. Besides Filter C which had already been tested, three further filters were designed. All three had the same specifications (32 taps, 40 Hz bandwidth) except that the method used to calculate their coefficients was different. A comparison of their frequency responses can be seen in Figure 7.

The characteristics of the filters can be seen in Appendix A: FIR Filter Characteristics while the results of the testing can be seen in Table 3.

Table 3: Final Filter Performance

Name	No. of Taps	Design Method	Azimuth Resolution	Peak Sidelobe Level	Integrated Sidelobe Level
Filter D	32	Kaiser	5.196 m	-14.276 dB	-12.070 dB
Filter E	32	Equiripple	4.932 m	-14.590 dB	-12.452 dB
Filter F	32	Linear	5.208m	-15.174 dB	-12.015 dB

It was noted in the processed outputs that aliasing had been introduced. Upon further investigation it appeared that this was introduced by the FIR filter when subsampling took place. The reason for this was that the stop band of the FIR filters would only attenuate the signal by approximately 20dB. This can be seen in Figure 35, Figure 37 and Figure 39. Frequency components which were higher than the Nyquist Sampling Frequency were therefore still present in the signal and these introduced the aliasing. The level of the aliased level (see Figure 8) was approximately 20dB lower than the focussed peak (seen in the centre of the diagram).

Filter F was chosen as the filter to be implemented. The reason for this was that it produced the lowest sidelobe level, as can be seen in Table 3. Although the azimuth resolution was worse than Filters D and E, this was not a problem as the final image would only be focussed to approximately 13m (see Section 5.1).

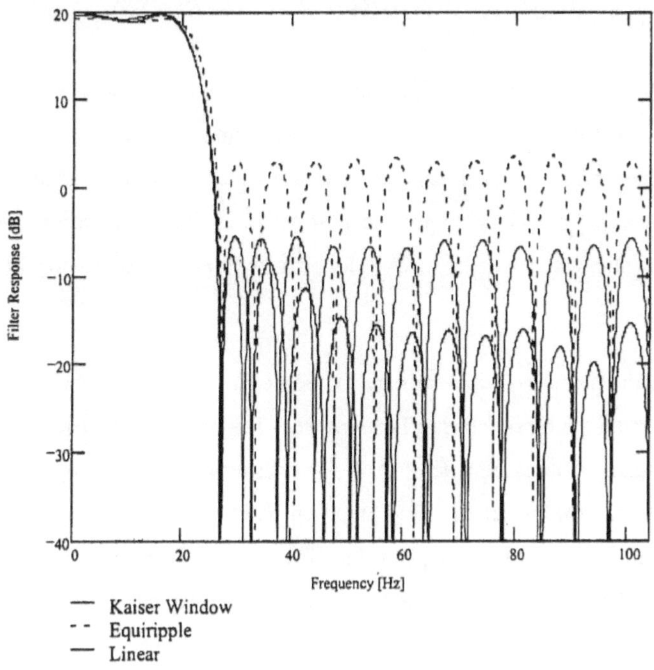

Figure 7: Filter Response Comparison

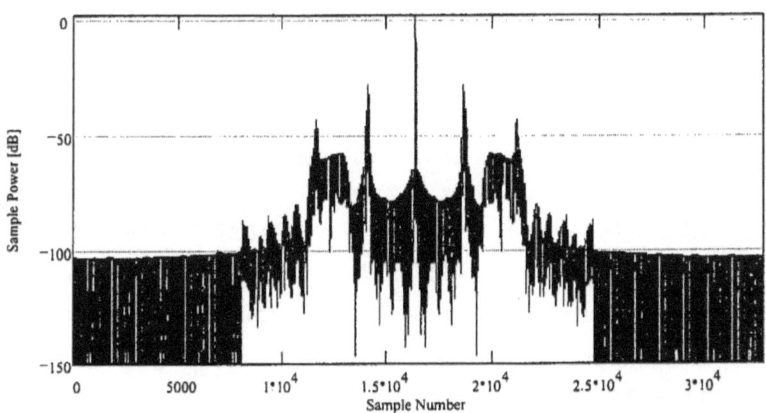

Figure 8: Processed SAR Data for Filter C

5.6   Algorithm Model

Once the details of the presummer and filter were decided upon, a VHDL algorithm model was written to test the effects of quantisation and precision. The MathCAD simulation made use of floating point values which were not available in FPGAs. The algorithm model had to provide a means for testing the precision needed when storing intermediate results as well the bit growth encountered when presumming and filtering.

Before the model could be written, the expected bit widths of the data at various stages in the processing had to be calculated. The presummer operated on eight bit values and presummed three of them for each result. Adding 3 eight bit numbers resulted in a ten bit number if no precision was to be lost. The presummer output was therefore set at ten bits per value. The bit growth in the FIR filter could be calculated as follows: The data to be operated on was ten bits wide. The coefficients were each eight bits wide. Thus every multiplication in the FIR filter produces an 18 bit result. There were 32 taps so 32 eighteen bit numbers were to be added. This would produce a 23 bit result. The internal precision of the FIR filter was therefore set at 23 bits. The data path widths can be seen in Figure 9.

The required output eight bits wide so the FIR filter output had to be divided to produce this. The division ratio was the presum gain (3) multiplied by the FIR filter gain (952). This produced the final eight bit value.

The VHDL algorithm model was written to read and write its data from disk. The output data would be used to test the results of the other models that were written. A model of the presummer was first coded and its output was manually verified. This data was then used as input to the prefilter model and once again the results were manually verified. Manual verification involved calculating the expected output and comparing it with the output produced by the model.

To test the effects of quantisation, the synthetic data which was generated in the MathCAD SAR processor was quantised to eight bits and processed by the algorithm model. This data was then imported back into the MathCAD processor and the image was focussed. The effects of quantisation were seen when comparing the outputs from the MathCAD and VHDL simulations, although the differences were minor. The peak sidelobe level of the MathCAD simulation was -14.279 dB, compared with the VHDL simulation value of -14.230 dB, while the integrated sidelobe level of the MathCAD simulation was -12.072 dB, compared with -12.033 dB. The width of the peak of the focussed target also increased by 0.23%. In a focussed image, these differences would not be noticeable to the naked eye. The reason why the quantisation effects in the final image were small was due to the large integration of the SAR processing.

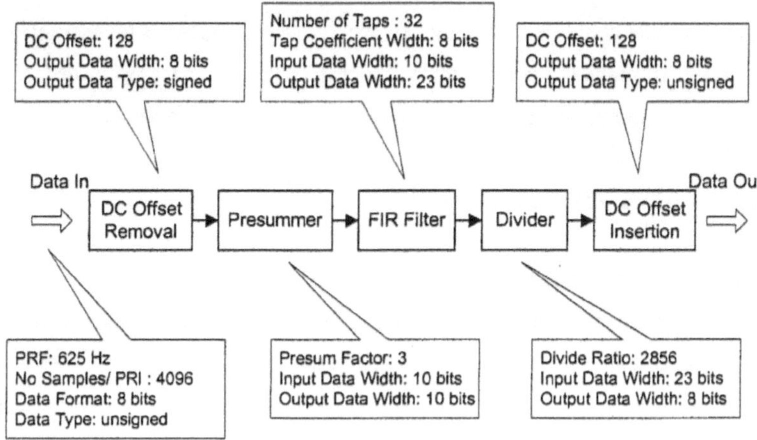

Figure 9: Algorithm Model Block Diagram

Chapter 6: Hardware Design

The preprocessor described above in Chapter 5: Preprocessor Design had to be implemented in hardware. Part of the objective of this book was to investigate the level of complexity of signal processing that could be achieved in dedicated hardware i.e. without the use of general purpose digital signal processors.

The simplest method of obtaining customised hardware was to make use of Field Programmable Gate Arrays (FPGAs). These devices contained thousands of digital logic gates that could be interconnected at will. Design software for these devices was used to produce a configuration file that could then be downloaded to the FPGA. This configuration file specified how these gates were to be connected.

6.1   Hardware Requirements

Before any hardware could be specified, the some basic calculations had to be performed to determine the input and output data rates and the amount of data to be stored. Since complex sampling was used, the I and Q values could be treated separately. This allowed a system to be designed to handle just the I values which could then be duplicated to handle the Q values. The following calculations are therefore only for the I values and are the same as those for the Q values.

For the presummer, one range line containing 4096 samples arrived every PRI. One PRI took 1.6ms (1/625 Hz) and so each sample had to be completed in 390ns. For the prefilter, since there was a skip factor of 4, a range line had to be output after 12 PRIs which took 19.2ms. Thus each prefiltered sample had to be completed in 4.6us (19.2ms/4096).

The calculations above gave the basic timing constraints of the system. Lower level timing could not be done at that time as such timing was dependent on the routing delays within the FPGA. To presum one sample, the sample had to be read from memory, added to another sample and the result then written back to memory.

Performing such an operation in 390ns seemed possible[4], considering that RAM access times were of the order of tens of nanoseconds and additions were of the same order. Similarly for each prefiltered sample, 32 RAM reads had to be performed as well as 32 multiply and adds. It therefore seemed, at a first look, as though these operations were possible in the allocated time.

Since the timing of each hardware operation was not accurately known, the possibility existed that the hardware would not be fast enough to meet the requirements above. To cope with this, methods were investigated to speed up the processing. These are detailed in Section 6.3.

6.2   Memory Overview

From the design detailed in Chapter 5: Preprocessor Design, it was decided to use a presummer before the prefilter. For the purposes of design, the prefilter and presummer were treated separately as they were mathematically separate. They could always be combined into a single FPGA at a later stage.

Both the presummer and prefilter needed RAM in which to store data. The presummer had to store the cumulative result of the presumming process before the final result was available. The prefilter had to store all the incoming data to be able to filter it as the data was to be filtered in azimuth, not range. Hence for a 32 tap filter, al least 32 range lines would need to be stored for each output row to be calculated.

The interface between the presummer and prefilter had to be determined. Two methods were evaluated. The first involved the use of separate memories for the prefilter and presummer while the second method used shared memory. The latter option was implemented.

---

[4] When the final implementation of the presummer was verified, it was able to perform at the required speed.

6.2.1 Separate Memories

In this method, the presummer and prefilter each had their own separate memories as can be seen in Figure 10. The first range line was read into the presummer and then stored in its RAM. The next range line was then read in and added to the stored result in RAM. This continued until the presummer had added the required number of range lines together. When this occurred, the presummer would output the presummed range line. The prefilter then read this presummed range line into its RAM. When sufficient range lines were in memory, the prefilter calculated its output and waited for more range lines to be read in.

<u>Advantage:</u> The advantage of this method was that the memory was cheaper than shared memory as conventional single ported SRAM could be used.

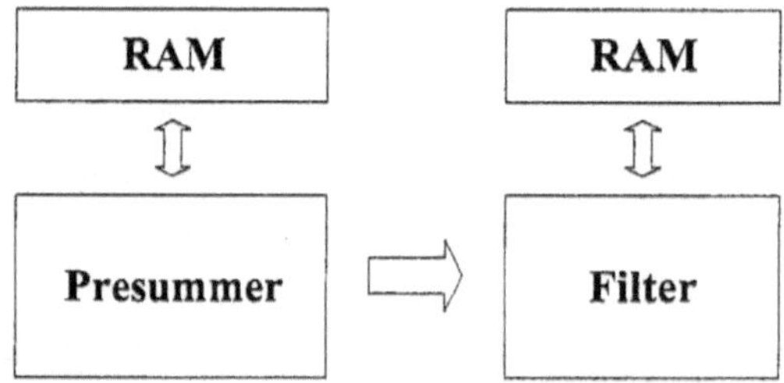

Figure 10: Block Diagram of Separate Memory Solution

<u>Disadvantage:</u> The disadvantages of this method were mostly due to the increased volume of data needing to be moved between presummer and prefilter. The prefilter would be slowed down with having to store incoming data in its own memory.

6.2.2 Shared Memory

In this method, the presummer and prefilter shared a block of dual-port RAM. This way, the presummer would write its temporary data to the address of the final presummed result. When the presummer finished summing the required number of rows, it would increment its address counter and begin writing to the next memory location. The result from the row just calculated would be left in place in memory. A block diagram of this solution can be seen in Figure 11.

The presummer would signal the prefilter when each new presummed row had been written to RAM. The prefilter would wait until the correct number of rows had been written before commencing with its prefiltering.

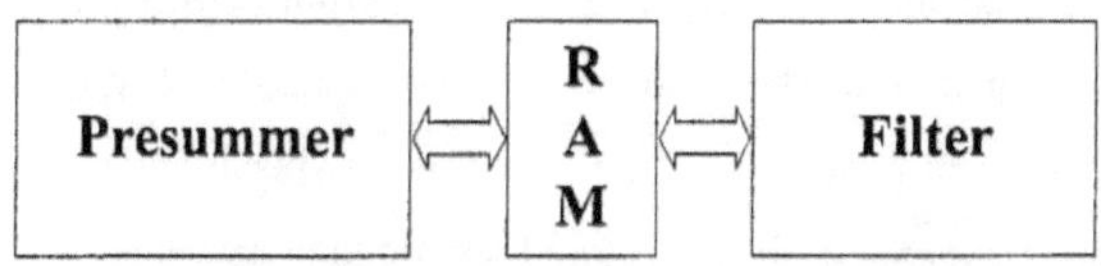

Figure 11: Block Diagram of Shared Memory Solution

<u>Advantages:</u> The advantage of this method was due to the simple data interface between the presummer and prefilter. The prefilter did not require additional overhead to store new incoming data which, in turn, increased the speed at which it could operate.

<u>Disadvantages:</u> The primary disadvantage of the shared RAM was the cost. Dual-ported RAM was more expensive than single-port RAM.

6.2.3   Memory Organisation

Incoming data could have been stored in memory in two ways: Range or Azimuth. If the data was stored in range, consecutive memory locations would hold the same range line. If the data was stored in azimuth then consecutive memory locations would hold the same range bin but from different range lines. These methods can be seen in Figure 12 and Figure 13.

It was not yet known how many parallel filters would be required to satisfy the processing requirements. It was therefore important that both of these memory organisations could be expanded or divided to suit a variable number of filters. Storing the data in range or azimuth made no difference to the expandability of the system as it was feasible to expand either memory organisation.

During the early stages of design, the RAM which was chosen featured an internal address counter. By using this internal address counter, the access time of the RAM was reduced. It was originally thought that the data should be stored in such a way that the prefilter (which was the more time critical of the two components) could make use of this counter to improve its speed. It was for this reason that it was decided to store the data in azimuth. Upon further investigation it became clear that using the internal address counters in the RAM would not work as the counter was not able to wrap around. The wrap around was required so that consecutive samples could be read from a single azimuth line. Since either memory organisation could be used, the orientation of the data stored remained in azimuth.

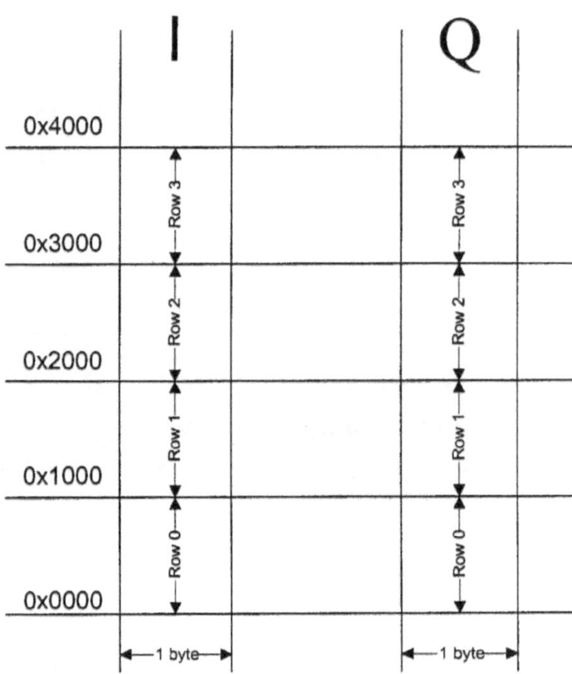

Figure 12: Memory Organisation – Data Stored in Range

6.2.4 Memory Requirements

At minimum, 32 range lines had to be stored so that the prefilter could process and output one range line, since it made use of a 32 tap filter in the azimuth direction. As all 32 range lines were required during the processing, data storage for more than 32 range lines was required to allow the presummer to continue storing new range lines while the prefilter processed its data. The number of range lines stored was required to be a power of 2 since that would allow address counters to roll over at the correct values. This was necessary as only a set number of PRIs could be stored and there was no limit on the number of incoming range lines. It was decided that storage space for 64 range lines would be made available since that was the next possible value after 32.

The width of the data memory was also considered. The incoming data from the radar was 8 bits wide. Adding three 8 bit numbers resulted in a 10 bit number, assuming an overflow was not allowed. It was therefore decided that 10 bit memory was to be used. This prevented the loss of any dynamic range due to overflow.

The total amount of RAM required was 512K x 10 bits. This number was decided upon as follows: 64 PRIs, each of 4096 complex samples = 64 * 4096 * 2 = 512K.

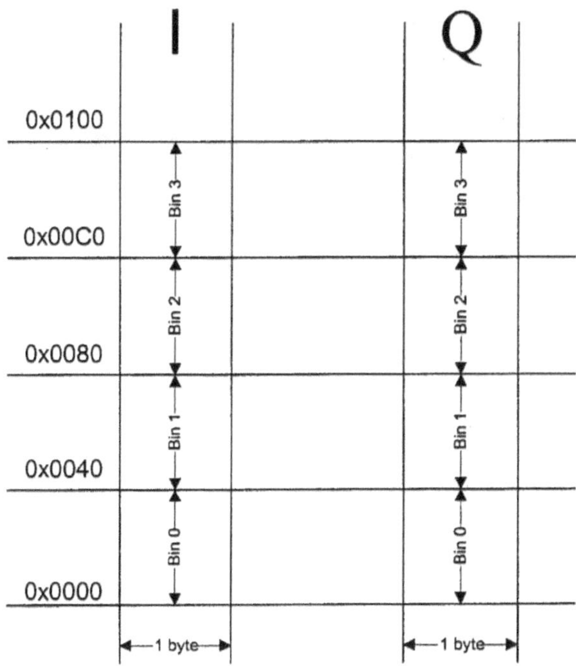

Figure 13: Memory Organisation – Data Stored in Azimuth

6.2.5   Memory Selection

Two types of Dual Ported RAM were available at design time: Synchronous and Asynchronous. The latter was the more common variety. To generate the precise timing signals required to access asynchronous RAM from an FPGA usually required the use of external programmable delay lines, unless multiple clock cycles were to be used to generate the required waveforms. These delay lines added extra complexity to the circuit, as well as an increased chip count.

Since synchronous design was the preferred approach in FPGA design, synchronous RAM was considered as an alternative. It appeared that synchronous RAM could be interfaced directly to the FPGA and still provide single clock cycle accesses. Further investigation took place to determine which devices were available.

In an attempt to minimise the chip count, high capacity RAM chips were sought. Cypress Semiconductor were going to produce a device which suited the needs of the radar. This was their CY7C09099 which was available in 128Kx8. It appeared at the time that the minimum width of available devices was 8 bits. This necessitated using two devices in parallel to achieve the required 10 bit data bus width. Wasting the 6 bits was unavoidable. At design time, this device was sampling and should have been available at the end of 1998.

6.2.6   VHDL Memory Model

Once the decision to use this device was made, the author attempted to locate a VHDL model for it. This model would be used in the functional model as well as in the simulation of the final FPGA. A suitable model could not be found and so it was decided to write one.

The model was a functional model and therefore contained no timing information, although this could have been added if required. The data for the model was obtained from a preliminary data sheet, since the final data sheets were not available.

The model differed from the data sheet in one area. The width of the data bus was increased from 8 bits to 10 bits. The reason for doing this was purely to increase its simulation performance. Even though the data was only 8 bits wide, each memory location required 32 bits to store because the value was stored as an integer. By increasing the model's data bus width to 10 bits, the memory required by RAM simulation was halved. This also increased the speed at which the RAM simulated.

6.3　Hardware Expandability

As described in Section 6.1, the expandability of the system was critical to its functioning, especially since the final operating speed of the hardware was not known before it was designed.

The simplest method of improving speed was to use parallel processes. This applied particularly to the FIR filters. Besides having two FIR filters (one for I values and the other for Q values) it may have been necessary to have multiple parallel FIR filters for processing the data. Since the filtering was done in azimuth, the data could be split in range. For example if there were two I data filters, one could filter the first half of the range bins while the other would filter the second half. Each filter would then have twice the amount of time to process the data and so its operating speed could be halved.

Both methods of memory organisation supported an increase in the number of filters. Each filter would require its own memory from where it could read its input data. The algorithm used by the presummer to calculate the position where the data was stored would have had to be improved. This would have been simple with memory mapping techniques.

A larger problem, should the system have required expansion, was to preserve the position in the PRI of samples output from the different filters. The design of the filters was to output their result for each range bin once it was processed. This would obviously not have worked if more than one filter were writing output samples at the same time. Samples from non-consecutive range bins could be output at the same time, thus mixing their order in the range line. Two solutions were proposed although neither had to be implemented since the filters were fast enough to process a complete range line I nthe required time.

6.3.1   Multiple Output FIFOs

This method made use of a FIFO for each filter coupled with some external control hardware. Once the filter had processed its portion of a range line and written the output data to its FIFO, it would have signalled the controller that it had completed its portion of the range line processing. The controller would then have read the contents of the FIFOs in the correct order and placed the processed data in a large output FIFO. The data in this FIFO would then have been in the correct order, as required.

Advantages: This method was the faster of the two in that the filters were required only to filter the data. The filters performed no data movement besides that required during the filtering.

Disadvantage: This method increased the chip count would therefore have been more expensive to implement.

6.3.2   Writeback to RAM

In this method, the prefilter would have written the processed data back to the RAM. Once the first filter had processed its portion of the range line, it would write the processed data to the output FIFO. On completion, the filter would signal the next filter to do the same. In this way, the data would be output in the correct order.

Advantage: This method was the cheaper solution as no extra ICs were required.

Disadvantages: This method was slower than using multiple FIFOs because the filters had to write the processed data back to RAM when they could have been reading new data. They would also have had to write the processed data to the FIFOs during the time they could have been processing. This would have resulted in a slower filter.

6.4   External Interface

Since the presummer and prefilter were not designed for standalone operation, it was important to confirm the specifications of the hardware that would interface with the presummer and prefilter. A block diagram can be seen in Figure 14.

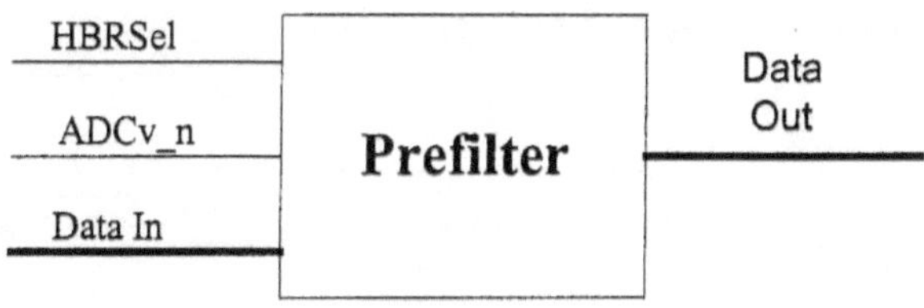

Figure 14: Top Level Block Diagram of the Prefilter

The two main control signals to the presummer were HBRSel and ADCV_n. The former signal was made active 100ns before the ADC started sampling a new range line. The ADCV_n line was then clocked every time a new sample was placed on the data bus. The ADCV_n line was active low. The processed data had to be output to a FIFO.

The I and Q channels of the ADC data bus were each eight bits wide. The data appearing on this bus was unsigned integers with a range from 0 to 255. The data incorporated a DC offset of 128.

The output data was to be buffered by a FIFO so that it could be accessed at a different rate to the prefilter output data rate. The format of the output data was the same as the input data: unsigned integers in the range of 0 to 255 with a DC offset of 128.

Chapter 7: Presummer Design

In keeping with the principles of RASSP, once the presummer was modelled on an algorithmic level, a functional model was then written. Once its operation was verified, the final implementation was coded. A diagram of the design steps regarding the models used can be found in Figure 15.

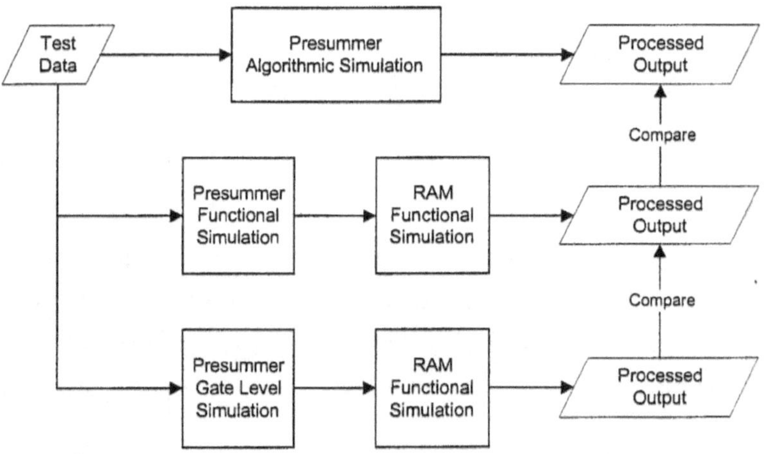

Figure 15: Presummer Model Overview

7.1   Functional Model

The algorithmic model developed in Chapter 5: Preprocessor Design provided a means of verification for any other models that were developed. Before the final implementation could be started, a functional model had to be written. This model had to behave in the same manner as the final implementation but did not need to be synthesisable. The purpose of this model was to verify the interaction between the presummer, RAM and prefilter.

7.1.1 Model Functionality

The VHDL model had to be able to interact with the RAM and FIFO models to be able to perform a system level simulation. The model also had to perform a presumming function of the incoming data. The only difference between this model and the final implementation was that it could not be synthesised into a FPGA.

The functional model contained no routing delay timing. If an output changed logic levels on a rising clock edge, that change would appear on the clock edge in the model, unlike a real FPGA where it would only occur a few nanoseconds after the clock edge. Another example of this lack of latency was in the addition and multiplication operations. These occurred instantly in the model, unlike in a FPGA. Since the entire design was synchronous, these did not present any problems as all operations took place on a clock edge and didn't rely on the when in the previous clock cycle the operation finished.

7.1.2 Presummer Interface

The first task during development of this model was to define the external interface. A number of pins were required to allow the device to interface with the RAM, external radar components and the prefilter. These pins are described in Table 4. More detail on the FIFO and RAM pins can be obtained from the relevant data sheets.

Table 4: Presummer Interface Pins

Pin	Description
FifoDataI, FifoDataQ	FIFO Data Bus (I & Q Channels). These were each 8 bits wide
FifoWEn1_n, FifoWEn2	FIFO Write Enable. Both need to be active to allow a write on the next rising edge of the FIFO Write Clock.
FifoREn1_n, FifoREn2_n	FIFO Read Enable. Both need to be active to allow a read on the next rising edge of the FIFO Read Clock
FifoEFI_n, FifoEFQ_n	FIFO Empty Flags (I & Q Channels). These signals are active when the corresponding FIFO is empty.
FifoRs_n	FIFO Asynchronous Reset

FifoOE_n	FIFO Output Enable
RamAddr	RAM Address Bus
RamADS_n	RAM Address Strobe. When active, the value on the RAM address bus is latched into the RAM on the rising edge of the RAM clock.
RamCE	RAM Chip Enable
RamCntEn_n	RAM Address Counter Enable. When active, the RAM's internal address counter is incremented on each rising edge of the RAM clock.
RamCntRst_n	RAM Address Counter Reset
RamDataI, RamDataQ	RAM Data Bus (I & Q Channels)
RamOE_n	RAM Output Enable
RAMRnW	RAM Read / Write Strobe
RAMPipenFT	RAM Pipeline / Flow Through Strobe. This toggles the RAM chip between pipeline and flow through modes.
Clk	System Clock
ClkTC	Timing Card Clock.
HBRSel	High Bitrate Recorder Select Signal
ADCv_n	ADC Data Valid Strobe
Reset_n	Asynchronous Master Reset
PSRowDone	Output to prefilter. Active for 1 clock period at the end of each presummed PRI.

7.1.3 Model Overview

Before explaining the workings of the presummer, the composition of the RAM address needs to be explained. A simple method of generating the correct RAM address was required to allow easy access to consecutive range bins and range lines without having to reload the address counters. The simplest method of doing this was to divide the address counter into two counters, a range bin counter and a range line counter. This can be seen in Figure 16. Every time the range bin counter was incremented, the next range bin of the selected range line would be accessed. Likewise, the same range bin from the next range line would be accessed if the range line counter was incremented. This is shown in Figure 17.

The range bin counter was actually comprised of two counters: "ColCounterR" and "ColCounterW" in the source code. The first counter was the range bin counter for the RAM's read operations while the latter was the range bin counter for the RAM's write operations. The use of two counters was unnecessary. The reason for their inclusion was that it was originally thought that a number of samples would be read and processed before being written back to RAM. Since the processed results would be written to the same address as the data which was retireved, the same sequence of RAM addresses had to be generated a second time. Using two counters were the easiest way of performing this. The two counters would initially be set equal to each other. A multiplexer would first select the "Read" counter. After the required number of samples were read and the counter incremented, the multiplexer would switch to the "Write" counter. The initial value of this counter would be the same as that of the "Read" counter. After the required number of write operations had been performed, the two counters would again be equal and the multiplexer would switch back to the "Read" counter.

Since only a single sample was processed at a time, this system could have been discarded but it allowed for future expansion and did not require much extra logic.

The MSB of the RAM address was used as a chip enable signal for the RAM. This allowed for the correct RAM chip to be selected for a given address.

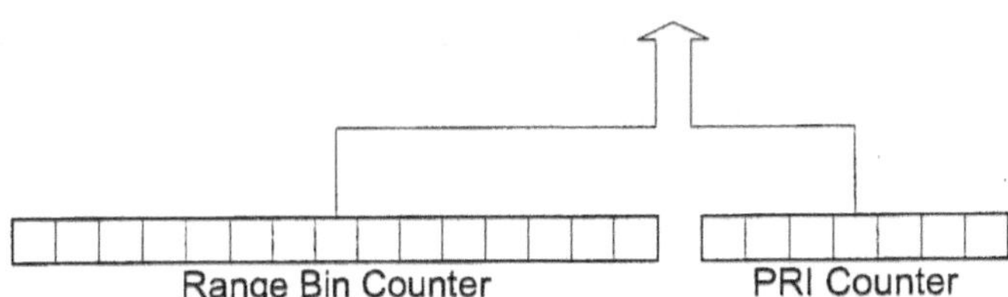

Figure 16: RAM Address Counter

The model used a state machine since it was the easiest method of sequencing the necessary logic. A block diagram of the presummer can be found in Figure 18.

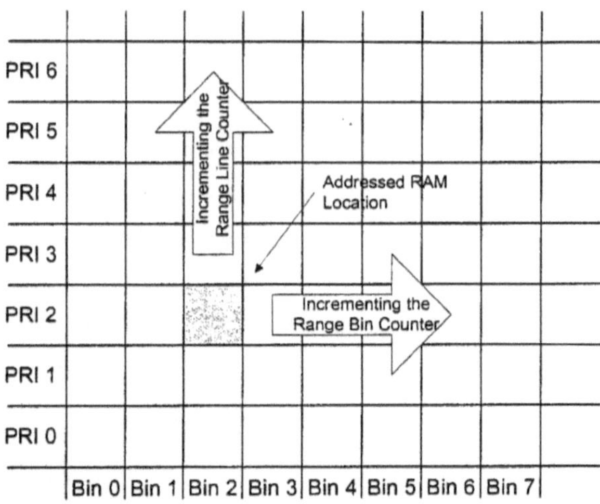

Figure 17: Effects on RAM Accesses from RAM Counter Increments

The operation of the presummer was as follows. The rising edge of HBRSel indicated that a new range line was about to be sampled. This caused the presummer to reset the FIFO to ensure that the position in the PRI of the new data was preserved as the first value read from the FIFO was assumed to be range bin 0. The internal counters in the presummer were also reset.

Once the ADC started sampling a range line, its data was written to the input FIFOs on the falling edge of ADCv_n. When the presummer detected that the FIFOs were not empty, it read a sample from them. At the same time it read the corresponding sample from memory. If this was the first range line of the three to be summed (the presum counter equalled zero), the FIFO sample would be stored in RAM. If not, the FIFO sample would be added to the RAM sample and the result written to RAM.

The range bin counter was incremented after each sample was processed. The presum counter was incremented every time the rising edge of HBRSel was detected. If this counter equalled three then the range line counter was also incremented the next presummed line was about to begin.

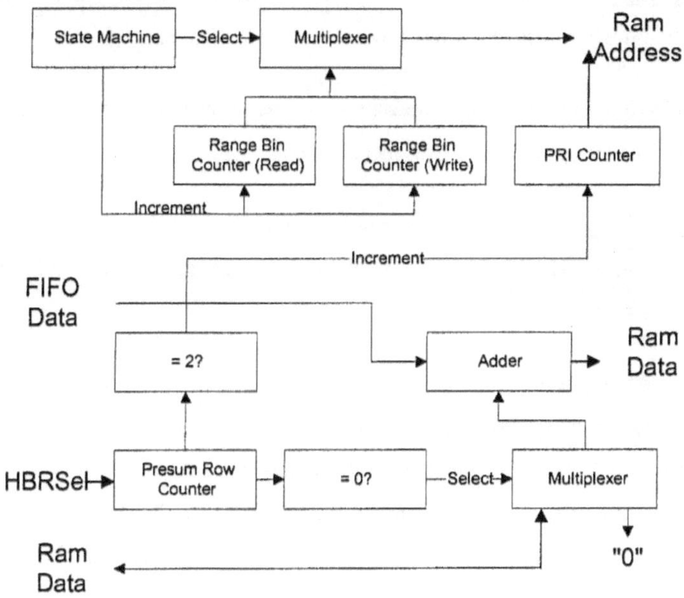

Figure 18: Block Diagram of Presummer

7.1.4   State Machine

A state machine was written to control the presummer. This was done as it was the simplest way of providing the required sequencing of operations. A block diagram of the state machine can be seen in Figure 19. A description of the states follows below.

StateReset: This was the reset state. It cleared all the counters, reset the FIFOs and the RAM signals.

StateIdle: This was the idle state. The state machine remained in this state while there are no samples in the FIFO.

StateRead: This was the read state. In this state, data was read from the FIFO and the RAM. The registers for holding this data were enabled to allow the data to be stored on the next rising edge of the clock.

StateWait: This state was a wait state. It was required as the synchronous RAM required it when switching from a read to a write operation.

StateWrite: This was the write state. The presummed data was written back to RAM. The range bin counter was incremented.

StateIncCntrs: This was the increment counters state and was entered when the rising edge of HBRSel was detected. In this state the presum and range line counters were incremented.

7.1.5   Verification

Once the model was written, it had to be verified. To do this, a testbench was written which provided stimulus to the inputs of the presummer. The stimulus emulated the inputs to the presummer from rest of the radar namely the ADC and input FIFOs. A block diagram of the testbench can be seen in Figure 20.

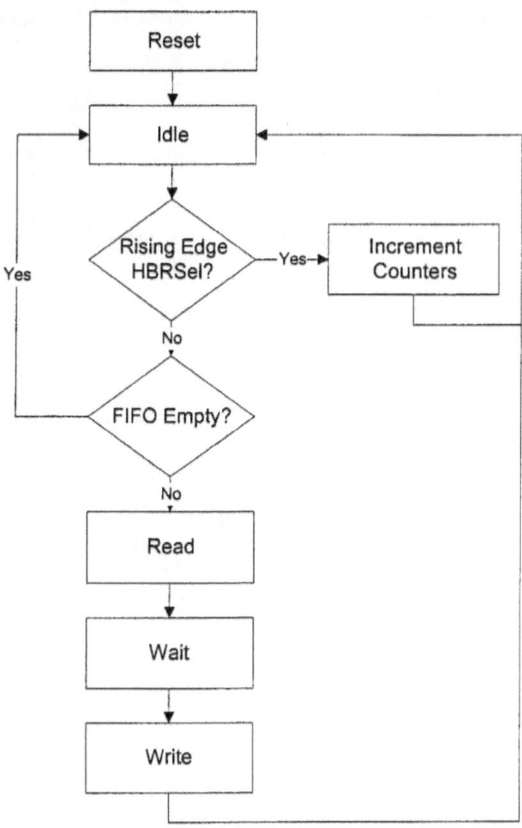

Figure 19: Presummer State Machine for Functional Model

At the beginning of each PRI, the testbench would cause the HBRSel signal to go high, indicating that the ADC was about to begin sampling. One hundred nanoseconds later, the ADCV_n signal would be pulled low, indicating that the first sample was available on the ADC data bus. The presummer would cause this sample to be written to the FIFO. This was modelled in the testbench by incrementing a counter which represented the number of samples in the FIFO. If the counter was not equal to zero, the testbench would pull the FifoEFI_n and FifoEFQ_n signals high, indicating to the presummer that the FIFOs were not empty. The presummer would then begin processing by requesting a read operation from the FIFOs. The testbench handled this by reading data from an input file every time a read operation was requested. At the same time, the counter which counted the number of samples in the FIFO was decremented.

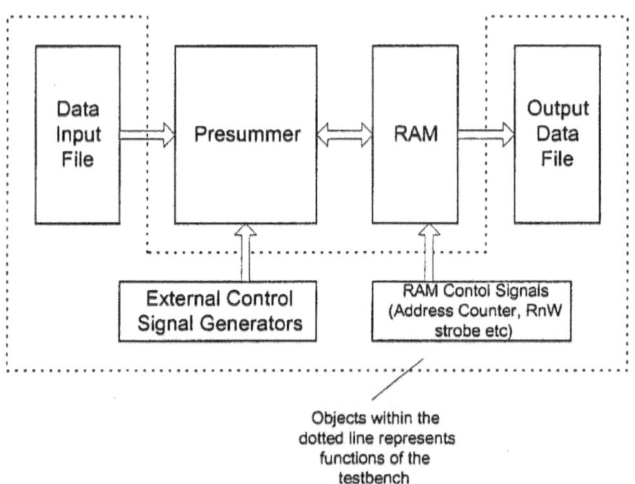

Figure 20: Presummer Testbench

The testbench was also responsible for writing presummed range lines to a disk for later analysis. The presummer indicated to the prefilter that a complete range line had been presummed by making the PSRowDone line active for one clock cycle. The simplest way of accessing this presummed line was the same way that the prefilter did so: using the second port of the dual port RAM. The testbench contained a range line and range bin counter identical to those explained in 0. Every time PSRowDone was made active, the testbench read a presummed range line from RAM and wrote it to disk.

Using files for the input and output data simplified the verification process. The same data that was used for the algorithmic simulation was sent through the presummer. The results were then compared and the presummer was validated.

7.2 Final Implementation

The functional model for the presummer provided much of the framework for the final implementation. A number of changes were made but these were mostly in an attempt to increase the operating speed.

7.2.1 State Machine Encoding

The same state machine was used for the implementation as for the functional model, except for two differences. The first is that an extra wait state was added to account for the pipelining in the LUT. The revised state machine can be seen in Figure 21. The second difference was the encoding style which was changed to a one hot encoding. The encoding of the state machine refers to how each state was represented at a bit level. There are two main encoding methods: Binary and one hot encoding.

7.2.1.1 Binary Encoding

The number of bits required to represent n states using binary encoding is given by the base 2 logarithm of the number of states. Thus representing four states requires two bits. Each bit is stored in a flip flop. A possible encoding of four states is:

State 1	"00"
State 2	"01"
State 3	"10"
State 4	"11"

The binary representation could have used a Gray Code. The advantage of the Gray Code is that only one bit changes at a time. This reduces the possibility of glitches which would occur when more than one flip flop didn't change value at the same time. For example, if a state machine changed from "01" to "10", two intermediate outputs are possible, "00" and "11". If either of these two values were output, the state machine could jump to an incorrect or illegal state if the state bits are used asynchronously.

The logic required to generate the next state for a binary encoding is a function of all the state bits. These functions are generally high-fan-in functions [3] and the logic required to implement them is often complex.

Care must be taken to prevent the state machine from entering illegal states. This usually happens when the setup and hold times of the state bit registers are violated. It is a simple matter to force the state machine back into a legal state should it enter one.

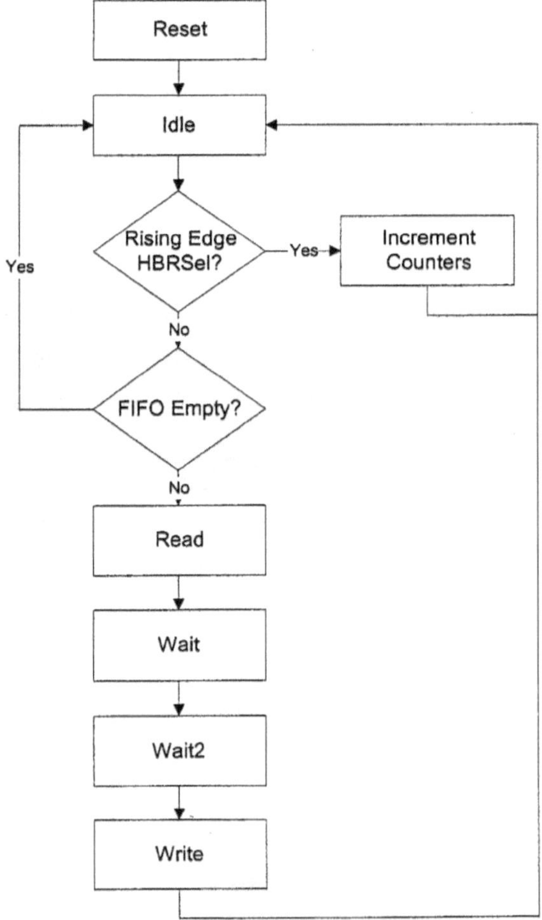

Figure 21: Presummer State Machine for Final Implementation

7.2.1.2   One Hot Encoding

One hot encoding dedicates an entire register to representing each state. The difference is that only one bit in each state register can be '1' at any time. A possible one hot state encoding of four states is as follows:

State 1	"0001"
State 2	"0010"
State 3	"0100"
State 4	"1000"

The advantage of the above encoding is in the amount of logic required for generating the next state. The next state generator for each state is a function of one state bit. By reducing the logic required for next state generation, the one hot encoding can increase the performance of the state machine over a binary encoded version.

The problem with this encoding method is the number of registers that are required, especially if there are a large number of states. Since FPGAs are rich in registers, using this encoding technique is best suited for these devices.

There are many more possible illegal states which a one hot encoded machine can enter. Since the one hot encoding assumes that only one bit is high in the state register at any one time, the next state generators cannot determine whether an illegal state has been entered. Assuming the setup and hold times on the state registers are not violated, the state machine should never enter one of these illegal states.

7.2.2   DC Offset Removal

Since the data sampled by the ADC had a DC offset of 128 added to it, this offset had to be removed before any processing could be done. Without removing the offset, no negative values would have been available and the results would be invalid. The removal of the DC offset could have been accomplished in one of two ways: Using a dedicated subtractor or a look up table (LUT).

Using a subtractor was considered but it was slower than the LUT equivalent. The FPGAs used contained limited amounts of internal memory and it was decided that since the resource was available, it should be used to speed up the design. The LUT used was 256 x 8 bits as the data received from the FIFO was used as the LUT address. The LUT was synchronous as the address was registered on each rising clock edge and the data was latched out a clock cycle later.

7.2.3   Pipelining

Pipelining is a method of increasing the throughput of a system by splitting it into smaller modules. To illustrate, consider a four input adder shown in Figure 22. Assume that each addition required time T to execute. The adder output would take 2T to calculate. Since this was a combinational circuit, the inputs A, B, C and D have to remain constant for the duration of the addition. The throughput of this adder is $1/(2T)$ and if it was used in a synchronous design, the maximum clock speed would be $1/(2T)$.

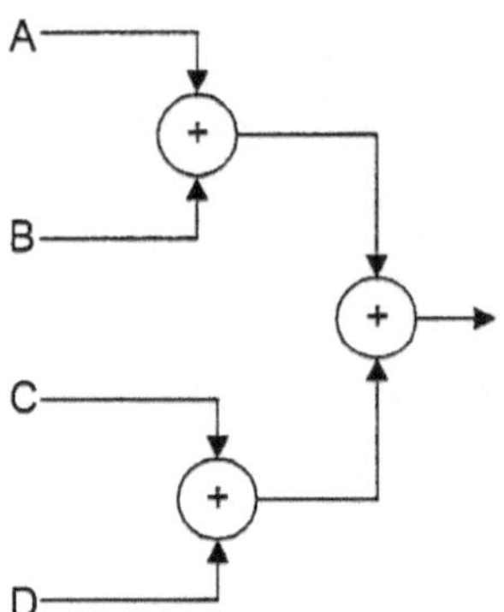

Figure 22: Non Pipelined Four Input Adder

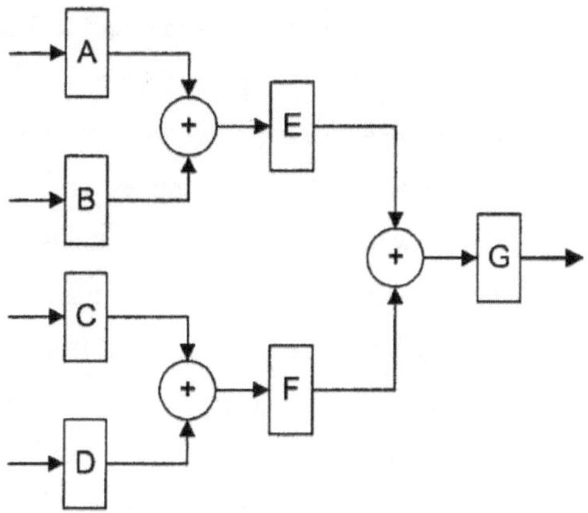

Figure 23: Pipelined Four Input Adder

Now consider a pipelined equivalent shown in Figure 23. At time 0, the input samples are clocked into the registers A, B, C and D. After time T, the sums A+B and C+D have completed and are clocked into registers E and F. At the same time, new data can be clocked into A, B, C and D. After time 2T, the sum of E+F has completed and is clocked into the output register G. The sums A+B and C+D have completed for the second set of inputs. The time taken to output calculate the sum of all four inputs is still 2T and the latency of the outputs is also 2T. The difference however is the throughput which has increased to 1/T since a new sample is available after every time T. This adder could therefore be clocked at 1/T.

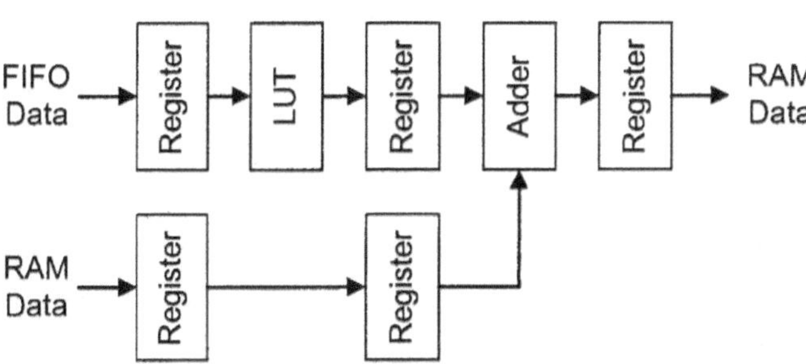

Figure 24: Presummer Data Path

The presummer was pipelined to increase its throughput. During the initial design stages, the length of the pipeline had to be decided upon. It was determined that the RAM interface would be the bottleneck of the system since the same data bus had to be used for reading and writing new data samples. The RAM required one clock cycle in order to switch between read and write operations. If one sample was read, processed and written back to RAM, the maximum utilisation of the RAM bus was 66% as one clock cycle in three would be wasted. Increasing the utilisation of the RAM bus required that a number of samples be read and written for each clock cycle lost. The function of the pipeline was therefore to maximise the use of this interface by allowing a number of samples to be read before the RAM had to perform write operations.

It turned out that the data arriving from the FIFO was sufficiently slow that the presummer could process each new sample as it arrived. Since the time between new samples arriving was much longer than the time it took to process one sample, the pipeline was made as short as possible so that the latency was minimised. The design however remained synchronous. A diagram of the pipelined data path can be seen in Figure 24. The data from the FIFO and RAM arrived at the same time but the FIFO data had a DC offset of 128 which was removed with a LUT. The LUT required a clock cycle to complete so an extra register was required in the RAM data path to synchronise it to the FIFO data. The adder used was pipelined and its result was also registered.

7.2.4 *Component Instantiation*

As the name implies, a VHDL synthesiser can synthesise logic for a number of given functions including multipliers and adders. Although the synthesis process produces functionally correct logic, it is not always optimal for what the designer intended. In the case of the presummer, two adders were required (I and Q channels). The VHDL synthesiser was capable of producing these adders when the addition operator was used in the source code, but faster adders could be obtained if adder components were instantiated.

The instantiated components were provided by Altera and conformed to the Library of Parameterised Modules (LPM) specification (see http://www.edif.org/lpmweb). LPM is an attempt by a number of EDA companies to produce a method of technology independent design by creating a standard library of components. The implementation of these components is left to the EDA tool vendors to create an optimal instantiation for the targeted device. If the designer then moves to another EDA tool vendor, the source does not need modification – the implementation is merely changed by the new EDA tool.

Instantiating the adder components allowed more control over the adder's performance. Most specifically, they provided a means of specifying the amount of pipelining which was to be used in the adder. This increased the throughput of the adder which was desirable. Another example of where component instantiation was used was in the generation of the LUTs. The reason for doing this was again to provide pipelining in the LUT.

The disadvantage of instantiating these components was that simulation models of them were only unavailable for the Altera software. The VHDL simulator did not support the LPM components and so the source code for the final implementation could only be simulated in Altera's graphical simulation environment (see Section 2.3.3). Since this simulator did not offer a full set of VHDL functions e.g. file I/O, the source code could not be simulated and checked by the testbench used in the functional simulation (see Section 7.2.5 below).

When instantiating components in the VHDL source code, it is important that simulation models of these components are provided. If the LPM components are to be used, make sure that the simulator supports them too. The whole simulation process cannot work if there are components which cannot be simulated.

7.2.5   Verification

Two aspects of the final implementation had to be verified: the functionality and the timing. Ideally, the functional verification would take place by simulating the synthesisable code and applying the testbench used in the functional simulation.

Once this was completed, the timing would be verified by using a model which incorporated the timing delays found in the physical device.

The functional verification described above could not be performed because the VHDL simulator used (Model Technologies' ModelTech ver 4.4j) did not have provide simulation models for the components which were instantiated. Some of functionality could be tested in Altera's graphical simulator while the remainder had to be performed when doing the timing verification. This was undesirable but unavoidable as another VHDL simulator with LPM support could not be obtained.

After the FPGA software had performed a place-and-route of the logic which the VHDL synthesiser had produced, it back annotated a VHDL model of the final FPGA implementation. This VHDL model contained all the timing delays that would be found in a physical FPGA. It was a gate level model where the characteristics of the individual gates were modelled. A disadvantage of this type of model was that all the signal names used in the synthesisable source are available for debugging.

This model was then compiled and substituted for the functional model in the presummer testbench. It was possible to do this as the back annotated model was completely simulatable. The required test data was used as input to the simulation and the results were compared with those obtained from the functional simulation. The back annotated model was therefore responsible for the verification of the device timing.

The execution time of the VHDL timing simulation was approximately 10 minutes for each millisecond simulated. The simulation was performed on an Intel PII-300MHz processor with 196MB RAM running Windows 95. The length of simulation was determined by how much data was to be processed. Since 64 range lines were to be stored in RAM, it was decided that at least that number had to be passed through the model to ensure that all the counters were working correctly. The result was that the simulation had to be run for a simulated time of 200ms which took approximately 2 days.

The speed of this timing simulation did not lend itself to the typical method of development where once a mistake was spotted, the entire design was recompiled and then simulated until all the errors are found and corrected. This would have been possible if the synthesisable source code was simulated as no place-and-route operation was required and the simulation speed would have been faster as the model would have been less detailed.

Debugging the simulation was equivalent to debugging a physical prototype except that a number of simulator features made the task easier. The simulator allowed traces to be plotted so that the values of individual signals could be monitored. Breakpoints were supported in the simulator so that the execution could be stopped at any point. The simulator could be run for a particular period of time or stepped through or over individual lines of VHDL source. Watch windows allowed the values of signals and variable to be monitored during this time. The only debugging that could have taken place if a physical prototype were used was that the outputs could be monitored with logic analyser. If any internal signals had to be checked, the design would have to have been recompiled and place-and-routed with the required signal routed to an output pin on the device.

7.2.6   Target Device

The presummer was implemented on an Altera EPF10K10ATC144-1 device. This was a 10000 gate FPGA in a 144pin Thin Quad Flat Package. The design occupied approximately 30% of the device capacity. According to the design software the maximum operating speed that device could operate at was approximately 50MHz.

Chapter 8: Prefilter Design

As was the case with the presummer, the same design methodology (RASSP) was used in designing the prefilter. A block diagram of the models used in the design process can be found in Figure 25.

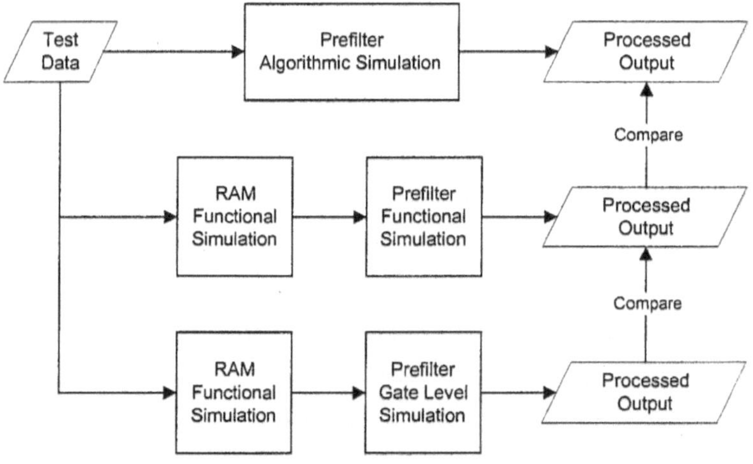

Figure 25: Prefilter Model Overview

8.1   The Functional Model

As with the presummer, the algorithmic simulation performed in Chapter 5: Preprocessor Design provided test data for verification of the functional model.

8.1.1   Model Functionality

Like the functional model of the presummer, the functional prefilter model was written to test the interface between it and the RAM, output FIFOs and presummer. The algorithmic simulation provided test data against which the output of the functional model was tested. This model was not synthesisable and provided no timing information.

8.1.2 Prefilter Interface

Before a model could be written, the prefilter interface had to be decided upon. The prefilter was required to interface with the presummer as it had to be signalled when a new presummer line had been written to RAM. The prefilter also had to be able to interface with the RAM as well as an output FIFO. A list of the input and output pins of the prefilter can be seen in Table 5.

Table 5: Prefilter Interface Pins

Pin	Description
FifoDataI, FifoDataQ	FIFO Output Data Bus (I & Q Channels). These were each 8 bits wide
FifoWEn1_n, FifoWEn2	FIFO Write Enable. Both need to be active to allow a write on the next rising edge of the FIFO Write Clock.
FifoRs_n	FIFO Asynchronous Reset
RamAddr	RAM Address Bus
RamADS_n	RAM Address Strobe. When active, the value on the RAM address bus is latched into the RAM on the rising edge of the RAM clock.
RamCE	RAM Chip Enable
RamCntEn_n	RAM Address Counter Enable. When active, the RAM's internal address counter is incremented on each rising edge of the RAM clock.
RamCntRst_n	RAM Address Counter Reset
RamDataI, RamDataQ	RAM Data Bus (I & Q Channels)
RamOE_n	RAM Output Enable
RAMRnW	RAM Read / Write Strobe
RAMPipenFT	RAM Pipeline / Flowthrough Strobe. This toggles the RAM chip between Pipeline and Flowthrough modes.
Clk	System Clock
Reset_n	Asynchronous Master Reset
PSRowInc	Output from presummer. Active for 1 clock period at the end of each presummed PRI.

8.1.3 Model Overview

A block diagram of the prefilter can be seen in Figure 26. The prefilter was controlled by a state machine.

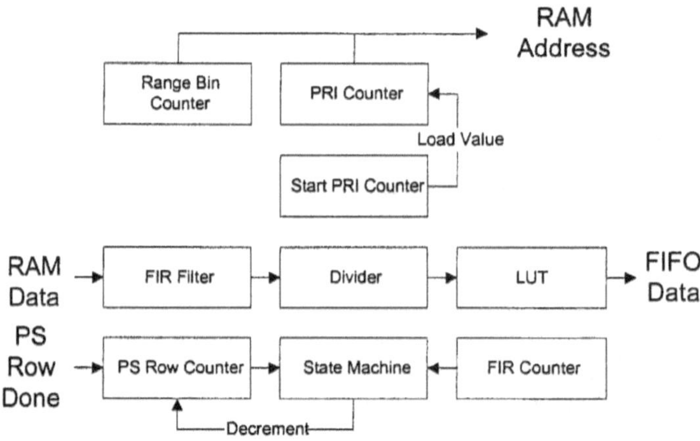

Figure 26: Block Diagram of Prefilter

The prefilter had a presum counter which was used to record the number of presummed lines in RAM at any time. This counter was incremented by one every time the presummer output a PSRowDone signal on that line. After 32 presummed range lines had been stored in RAM, the state machine would begin the processing.

The presummed data was read from RAM and input into the FIR filter. After 32 samples had been processed by the filter, the output was latched so that the FIR filter could continue processing a new set of data while the final output was being calculated.

The final output had to be in the form of an eight bit, unsigned integer with a DC offset of 128. In order to achieve this, the FIR filter output had to be divided by the sum of the magnitude of filter coefficients multiplied by the presum factor. This resulted in an output in the range –128 to 127. This value was then added to 128 to produce an unsigned integer in the range 0 to 255. This value was then written to the output FIFO.

Since only 64 range lines were stored, the data had to be wrapped around in memory. This was especially necessary since the presummer had to continue writing data to RAM while the prefilter was reading the 32 range lines required for its processing. For this reason, three counters were used for the RAM address. The first was a range bin counter (12 bits) while the second was a range line counter (6 bits). These were concatenated to provide the RAM address as in the presummer (see Figure 17 and Figure 16). A start sample counter (6 bits) was the third counter used and provided the reload value for the range line counter.

When the data from each new range bin was to be read into the FIR filter, the range line counter was preloaded with the value of the start counter. The range line counter was then incremented 32 times to read the required values from RAM. This counter would roll over at a count value of 63 so that the data could be wrapped around in memory. After 32 data values had been read, the range bin counter was incremented and the process repeated. In this way, all the required data could be read while the presummer continued to write new data to RAM. Note that since the prefilter had to produce a prefiltered range line every 12 PRIs, there would never be a situation where the presummer would overwrite data which had not been filtered.

Once a complete range line had been filtered, the presum counter was decremented by 4, since 4 was the skip factor. The remaining 28 range lines stored in RAM were required for the next range line filter.

8.1.4 *State Machine*

A state machine was used to control the prefilter and all its external outputs. The operation is described below and can be seen in Figure 27.

StateReset: This was the reset state. All the RAM address counters were reset.

StateIdle: This was the idle state. The state machine remained in this state until the presummer had written 32 range lines to RAM. When this occurred, the state machine would advance to the read state. The RAM address counters were reset in the idle state.

StateRead: This was the read state. The state machine remained in this state until 32 samples had been read from RAM into the FIR filter. This state used a down counter to count the number of clock cycles which occurred while in this state.

When the down counter reached zero, the state machine moved to the next state. A down counter was used as it was the most efficient method of waiting for a set period of time. The alternative was to create the same number of wait states as clock cycles to be waited. That would have been very inefficient and was not implemented.

StateIncCntrs: This was the increment counters state. It was entered at the end of a read and was used to increment the address counters and reload the range line counter.

StateDecPSRows: This was the decrement presummed rows state. It was entered at the end of processing a range line and was used to decrement the presum counter.

8.1.5   Verification

A testbench was written to read the data output by the presummer testbench and pass it through the prefilter. The data output by the prefilter was then written to disk to be compared with the algorithmic simulation results. A block diagram of the testbench can be seen in Figure 28.

On startup, the testbench would write the 64 ranges lines of data to the one port of the RAM, asserting the PSRowDone signal for one clock cycle at the end of each PRI written. When the prefilter detected that the required number of rows (32) had been written, it would read the data from the other RAM port, process it and output the result. The prefilter would assert the output FIFOs write enable signal when the processed sample was ready for output. The testbench used this signal to write the processed value to disk. These results were then compared with those obtained from the algorithmic simulation to verify the operation of the functional model.

The test data was prefiltered and the correct data was output.

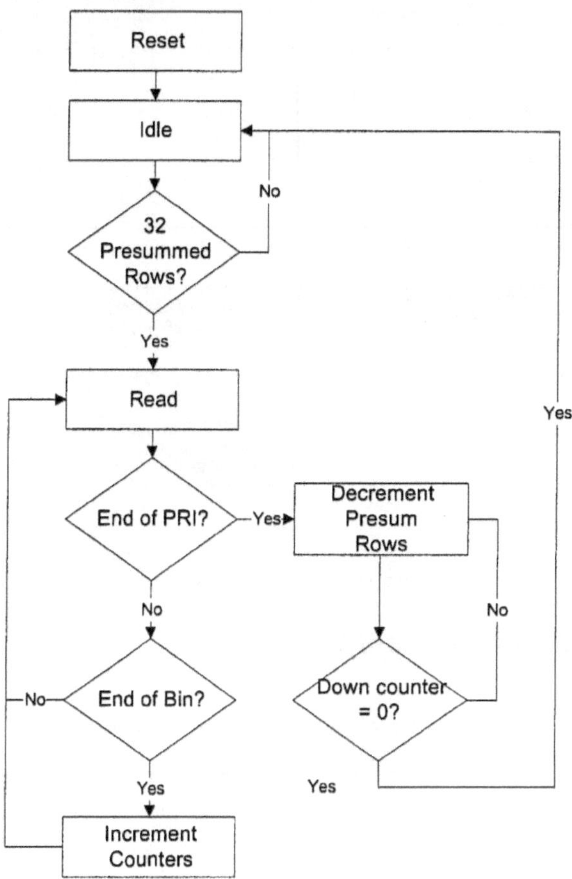

Figure 27: Prefilter State Machine

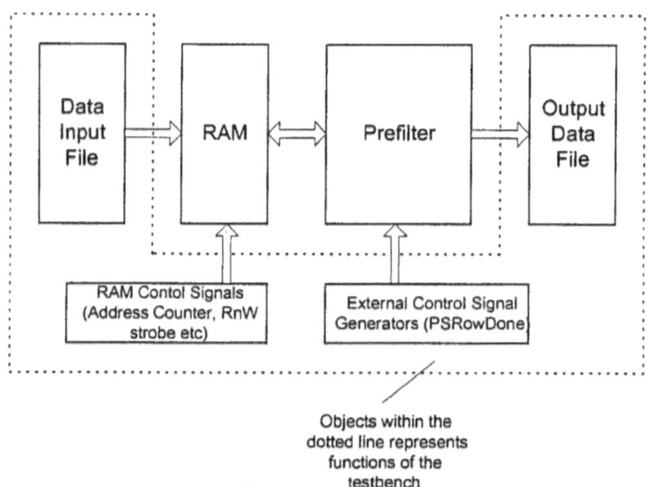

Figure 28: Prefilter Testbench

8.2 Final Implementation

The functional simulation provided much of the framework for the final implementation of the prefilter which also used a state machine for control. Many of the same methods that were used for improving the operating speed of the presummer were used for the prefilter. Descriptions of these can be found in Section 7.2.

8.2.1 State Machine

The same state machine that was used in the behavioural model was used in the final implementation. The only change to it was that one hot encoding (see Section 7.2.1.2) was used to increase its operating speed.

The down counter that was described in section 8.1.4 was also used to generate the output FIFO write enable signal and the register enable signal for the divider register. These signals were generated when the down counter reached certain predetermined values.

8.2.2 FIR Filter

A few options existed for implementing the FIR filter. The first was to use a FIR filter module written by Altera. This module claimed operation speeds of up to 100MHz, variable input data widths, output data widths and internal precision. The filter also had an option to include pipelining. The problem with this filter was that is was only available in 8, 16, 32 and 64 taps and the coefficients had to be either symmetric or anti-symmetric. The second option was to use the FIR filter module provided by Synopsys. After further investigation it turned out that a licence for this module was unavailable and so it could not be used. The last option was to write a FIR filter but this implementation would not have been an optimal solution. The module from Altera was chosen as the implementation that would be used. The filter coefficients had to be recalculated to for a filter length of 32.

The filter core was only available in AHDL, a proprietary hardware description language by Altera. This posed a problem in compiling and simulating the prefilter as Altera's MaxPlus2 software was the only software that could read AHDL. Since using this module provided the only real option for implementing a FIR filter, it had to be used.

Unlike the Synopsys FIR filter which could load new coefficients during its operation, the Altera FIR Filter's coefficients were specified at compile time. If the system was required to change filters during operation, it was possible to load the FPGA with a new precompiled configuration with different coefficients.

To optimise the FIR filter, Altera made use of LUT-based vector multipliers [2]. The coefficients were divided into partial products which were then added together. Performing addition operations were faster than multiplications. This resulted in a very fast FIR filter. The required coefficients were input to an Altera supplied program which calculated the partial products. The partial products were then linked into the design when the FIR filter module was instantiated.

Since the FIR filter was written in AHDL and the rest of the presummer was written in VHDL, a method of combining these had to be found. The solution was to use the graphical schematic entry tool in MaxPlus2. The required FIR filter components were instantiated and after the VHDL section was compiled, a schematic symbol was created for it. This was then connected to the FIR filter in the schematic editor. In this way, the two major components of the prefilter were combined into one entity.

Although the documentation [1] claims that the bit widths of the filter coefficients can be independently specified of the data bus width, this appears to be inaccurate. The initial design made use of ten bit data and eight bit coefficients. The FIR filter operated correctly when an impulse function was passed through it – the values of the coefficients were output. Any other input data produced an incorrect output on at least one of the filter tap outputs. It was thought that the problem was due to the internal precision (precision of the calculations) of the filter but this was excluded for two reasons: Firstly, when the internal precision was increased, the problem remained. Secondly, the values used for testing were too small for overflow to occur. No pattern seemed to exist which would predict which coefficient would cause the incorrect value to be output. The problem was finally solved by increasing the precision of the filter coefficients to ten bits. Although their values remained unchanged, the problem was solved. The cause of the problem is still not know.

8.2.3   Dividers

The output of the FIR filter was 23 bits wide to prevent loss of dynamic range or overflow. This output contained a gain associated with the filter coefficients as well as a gain introduced by the presumming. The presum gain was three, the number of lines that were presummed. The filter gain was equal to the sum of the absolute value of the coefficients. This equalled the maximum gain that the FIR filter could apply to any data stream. The filter gain for the coefficients used was 952 (see Appendix A: FIR Filter Characteristics for details on the coefficients). The FIR filter output therefore had to be divided by 2856 to scale the result down to eight bits.

Altera provided a divider core that was initially used. This core was configurable as the bit widths of the inputs and outputs could be modified, as well as the number of pipeline stages. During final testing it was discovered that the divider could only operate on unsigned values. Another solution had to be found.

A number of alternatives were examined. The first was to perform a partial fractional decomposition of the division by 2856 into a number of powers of 2. The values of a, b, c, d and e in Equation 5 were computed using a PBIL based search program written by Richard Lord which made use of the algorithm described in [6]. The number of partial fractions to use was variable but four seemed to give a good trade off between accuracy and the amount of logic required to implement. The final approximation used can be seen in Equation 6. By making use of divisors which were powers of two, the division could be performed with an arithmetic right shift operation.

$$\frac{1}{2856} \approx \frac{1}{2^a} + \frac{1}{2^b} + \frac{1}{2^c} + \frac{1}{2^d} + \cdots \qquad \text{Equation 5}$$

These partial fractions could then be added which was faster than a division operation. The error in the approximation was approximately 3×10^{-6}. The problem with the implementation of this was that truncation errors were introduced in the division. Since the representation of the data was in the form of integers, no fractional parts of the results were stored or used. This truncation error was compounded since it occurred in the calculation of each partial fraction. This resulted in incorrect values and an alternative solution was investigated.

$$\frac{1}{2856} \approx \frac{1}{2^{12}} + \frac{1}{2^{14}} + \frac{1}{2^{15}} + \frac{1}{2^{17}} \qquad \text{Equation 6}$$

The solution implemented made use of the unsigned divider provided by Altera. The data output from the FIR filter was examined to determine if it was positive or negative. The absolute value of the output was taken and this unsigned value was input to the divider. The output of the divider was then sent to two LUTs, one for positive values and one for negative values. The function of the LUT was to convert the divider output into the eight bit, unsigned value required for output. Two LUTs were required since different offsets were required for positive and negative values.

A multiplexer was used to connect the two LUTs outputs to the FIFO data port. The select signal for the multiplexer was controlled by the most significant bit of the FIR filter output. If it was a logic '1', the number was negative. This method worked correctly.

8.2.4   DC Offset

Since the original data had a DC offset of 128, this offset had to be reinstated before the data could be output. To do this, a LUT was used, as in the case of the presummer.

As described in Section 8.2.3, the divider could only operate on unsigned values. The absolute value of the numerator was used in the dividing process. Instead of providing an output in the range −128 to 127, the output range was 0 to 128. Since a DC offset had to be added to these values, it was decided to make use of two LUTs, one for negative numerators and the other for positive numerators. The LUTs were different as different offsets had to be added depending on the sign of the numerator.

The LUT for positive numerators was 127x8 bits. This LUT merely added the required 128 to the quotient to map the positive output values to the range of 128 to 255.

The LUT for negative numerators was a little more complex. The range of quotients was 0 to 128. The reason for this was that two's complement representation of integers has a larger range for negative number than positive ones. A LUT of 256x8 bits was required to hold the offset output values. There was no constant DC offset that was added to these values – the offset had to be equal to the negative of the input value added to the required DC offset of 128. The output range of 0 to 128 was therefore mapped to the range 128 to 0.

A multiplexer was used to select the required output from the positive and negative LUTs. The selection signal for the multiplexer was taken from the MSB of the FIR filter output. The MSB was the sign bit of the value. When it was '1', the number was negative.

8.2.5   Verification

The final implementation was verified in two steps. Its functionality was first tested in the Altera MaxPlus2 Environment. The timing was then tested using a back annotated VHDL model of the prefilter. This model was used in conjunction with the functional model testbench described in Section 8.1.5.

The prefilter design was large and the entire compilation process took a number of hours to compile and fit. The Altera software provided an option to compile the design for a functional simulation. This simulation was performed on the synthesised logic and no place-and-routing took place. This reduced the compilation time to under an hour which made the debugging process more feasible. The problem with this was that only the Altera graphical simulator could be used as no other simulator supported AHDL components. The Altera simulator did not support the use of testbenches. If VHDL simulation models had existed for all the components used, this method of verification would have been unnecessary as the VHDL source could have been simulated before being place-and-routed. Due to the size of the design, this simulation was time consuming. It took approximately 1 min to simulate 1us.

Once the functionality of the prefilter implementation had been verified, its timing had to be tested. The MaxPlus2 design software provided this information in a back annotated gate level VHDL model. This model was very large (approximately 18MB of VHDL source!). Simulation times were very slow due to the size and complexity of the model which included setup and hold time checks on the input signals. This simulation was performed on an Intel PII-300MHz with 196MB RAM and took approximately 24 hours to simulate 5ms of time. This was unacceptable as it would have taken approximately 60 days of simulation time to thoroughly test the timing of the entire design. The only aspect that was not tested in the timing model was the address counter overflows but these were verified in the functional verification.

The same input that was used in the functional model was to verify the final implementation timing model. The processed outputs were compared and were identical. The timing of the inputs to the FPGA were tested by the back annotated model, while the outputs to the RAM and FIFO were inspected visually. Traces of the signals were plotted and the setup and hold times were measured and verified.

8.2.6   Target Device

The prefilter was fitted to an Altera EPF10K100ARC240-1 device. This was the fastest 100000 gate device that Altera made at design time. The device was approximately 81% full. A larger capacity device should have been used if the design was likely to undergo modification, especially if pin locking was needed. Since this was not the case, however, the 100000 gate device was used.

According to the design software, the maximum registered clock speed that could be used was 44MHz. The slowest part of the design was the divider whose propogation delay was approximately 23ns.

The operating speed was more than adequate for the prefilter to operate correctly. If the design was to be produced on a large scale, the use of a slower device could have been investigated. Combining the presummer and prefilter onto one FPGA could also have been investigated as a means of reducing costs.

Chapter 9: Conclusions and Recommendations

The following conclusions were drawn from the work performed as described above.

It is impossible to validate the goals of RASSP from this case study. A comparison would have to be performed with the design of the same system using non-RASSP design techniques. What can be concluded is that Virtual Prototyping is a useful tool when designing digital circuits although it need not be used in every design. The overhead required in writing the models required needs to be weighed against the decrease in debugging time. This is particularly true of small designs.

The first important criterion for a successful system level simulation is that all the entities and components used must have VHDL simulation models. One of the larger problems encountered was that the VHDL source files could not be simulated by the VHDL simulator because certain components which were instantiated had no VHDL simulation models. If the source files could be simulated in the simulator, the debugging time would have been reduced as a VHDL simulator is more powerful and contains more features than the graphical simulators which accompany many of the FPGA design packages. For systems which employ more complex devices like DSPs and micro-controllers simulation models would have to be purchased as they have a long development time and omitting them from the simulation would defeat the purpose of the simulation.

Virtual prototyping has advantages in that the cost of debugging is small (excluding the billable time for those who are performing the debugging). Once an error is found, it can be corrected in software and the system simulated again. If the error was found in the physical prototype, it could possibly be corrected in software although often a hardware modification would be required.

Gate level simulations are impractical for large designs. The time required to simulate the design can be longer than the time required to build a physical prototype, as was the case in this case study. The functionality of the final simulation can be verified without using a gate level simulation if all the components used have simulation models, or their VHDL source code is available.

The use of FPGAs in DSP systems is definitely practical and excellent results can be obtained. The decision on whether to use an FPGA or dedicated DSP must be taken in light of the tasks to be performed although the following guidelines can be applied: Floating point operations are not suited to FPGAs as most of the available components only support integer operations. Multiplication and division operations are costly in terms of resource usage.

Although a seemingly obvious point, the architecture of a DSP is fixed, compared to the FPGA whose architecture is specified by the designer. A greater amount of flexibility is offered by the DSP when modifications are required. To modify the operation of an FPGA often requires the designer to make major architectural changes, unlike the DSP programmer who changes a few lines of source code. Having said this, the use of VHDL has progressed the design of FPGAs a long way down the road to supporting quick design modifications. If the synthesisable description of the FPGA is written at a high level, making changes in its operation is not much more complex than adding a few lines of VHDL code. For DSP type work, the designer is likely to specify the architecture of the FPGA at a low level so that the operating speed can be maximised. This is because since the lower the abstraction level of the synthesisable code, the more control the designer has over the synthesised result.

The majority of VHDL simulators on the market are event based simulators. Cycle based simulators are making their appearance with claims of 10x speed improvements over event driven simulators for gate level simulations. It would be interesting to test these claims as increasing simulator speeds could make gate level simulations of large systems feasible. Testing other simulators which ran on multiprocessor computers would further test the feasibility of gate level simulations.

Appendix A: FIR Filter Characteristics

This appendix details the characteristics of the different FIR filters tested and the results of their testing. The first three filters were created using the algorithm described in [16]. The first of the three filters was designed to operate with no presummer i.e. the sampling frequency was 625Hz and had 64 taps. A 32 tap equivalent could not be constructed since there were too few taps to specify a cutoff frequency of 20Hz. The second and third filters were used to compare the effects of 64 and 32 tap filters with a sampling frequency of 208.33Hz.

The remaining filters were constructed to determine the best 32 tap filter which would operate with a sampling frequency of 208.33Hz.

The coefficient values used for the testing can be found in Table 6 on page 91.

A.1   Filter A

The frequency response of this filter can be seen in Figure 29. The filter was designed to operate on data which had been sampled at 625Hz and has 64 taps. The an optimal method was used for designing the coefficients and can be found in [16]

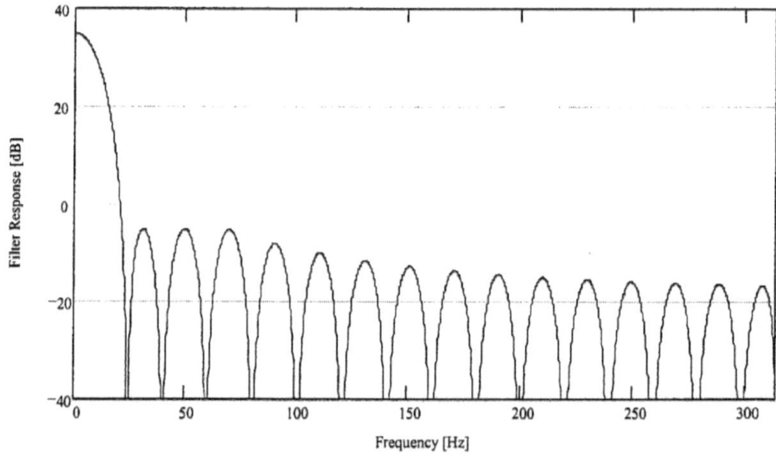

Figure 29: Frequency Response of Filter A

A graph of the filter tap coefficients can be seen Figure 30.

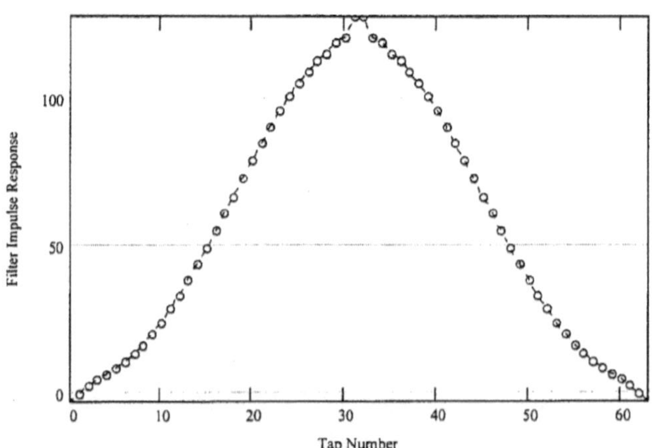

Figure 30: Coefficients of Filter A

A.2   Filter B

This filter was created using the same method as Filter A above. It also contained 64 taps but was designed to operate on data which was sampled at 208.33Hz. Its frequency response can be seen in Figure 31 and its coefficients can be seen in Figure 32

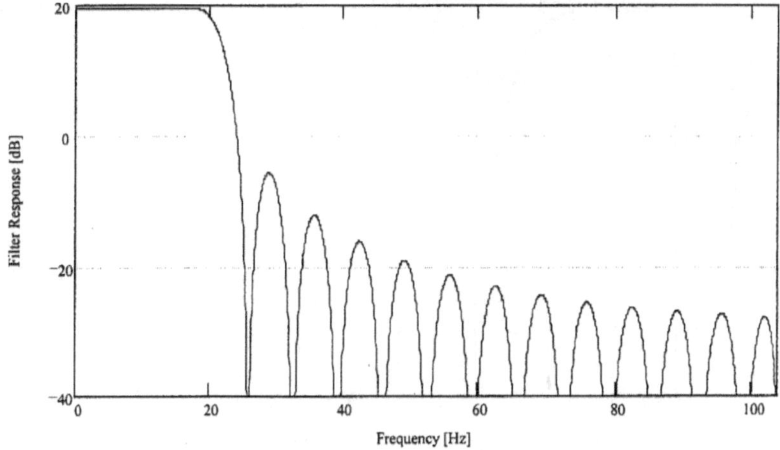

Figure 31: Frequency Response of Filter B

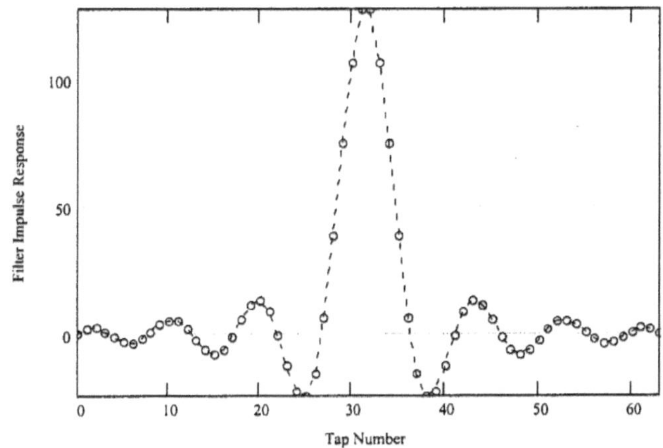

Figure 32: Coefficients of Filter B

A.3   Filter C

This filter was designed with the same method as filters A and B. It was designed to operate on data which was sampled at 208Hz but contained 32 taps. The frequency response can be seen in Figure 33 and the filter coefficients can be seen in Figure 34.

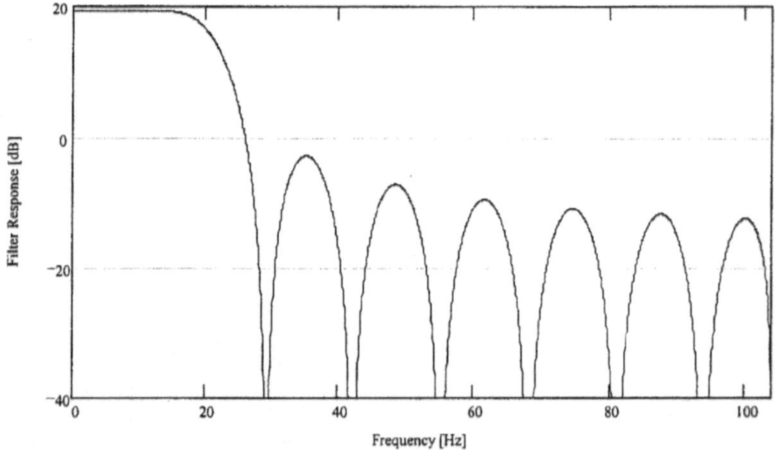

Figure 33: Frequency Response of Filter C

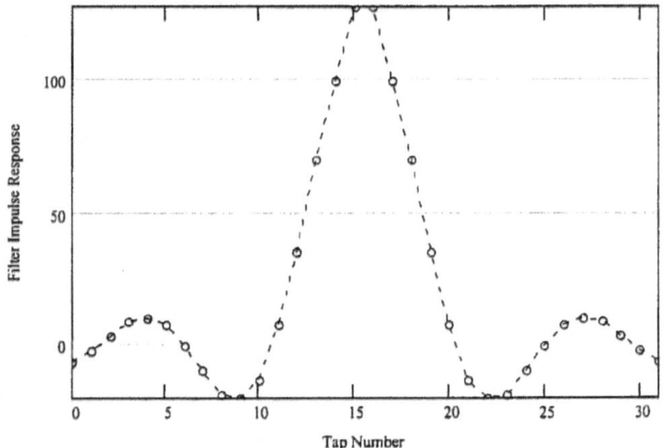

Figure 34: Coefficients of Filter C

A.4　　Filter D

This filter was designed using a Kaiser Window. It was a 32 tap filter designed to operate on data sampled at 208Hz. Its frequency response can be seen in Figure 35 and its filter coefficients in Figure 36

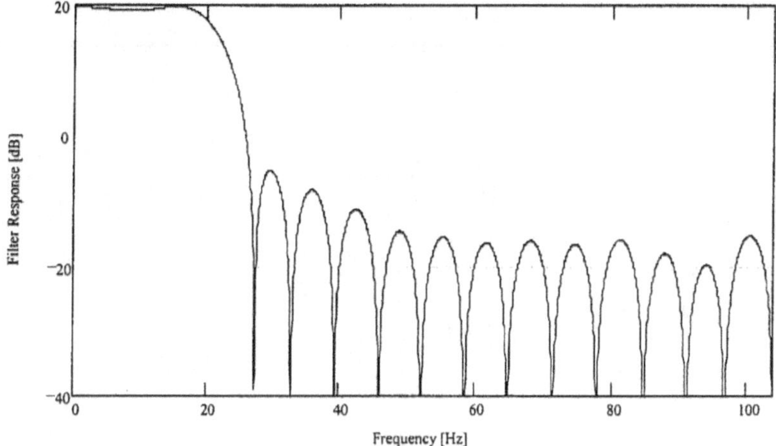

Figure 35: Frequency Response of Filter D

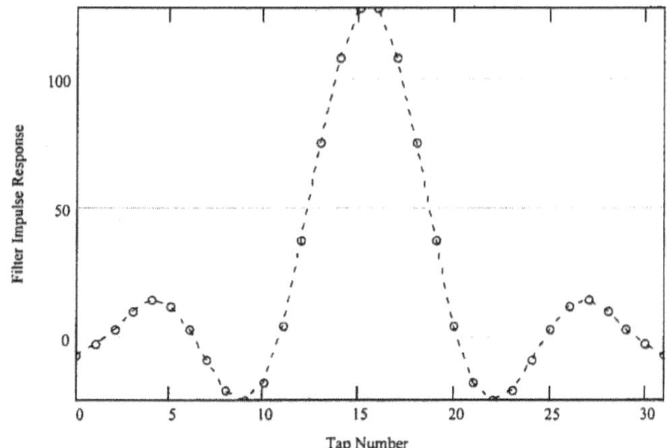

Figure 36: Coefficients of Filter D

A.5 Filter E

This filter was designed using an equiripple method. As can be seen from its frequency response in Figure 37, the sidelobes were all of equal height. It was a 32 tap filter designed to operate on data sampled at 208Hz. Its filter coefficients are shown in Figure 38

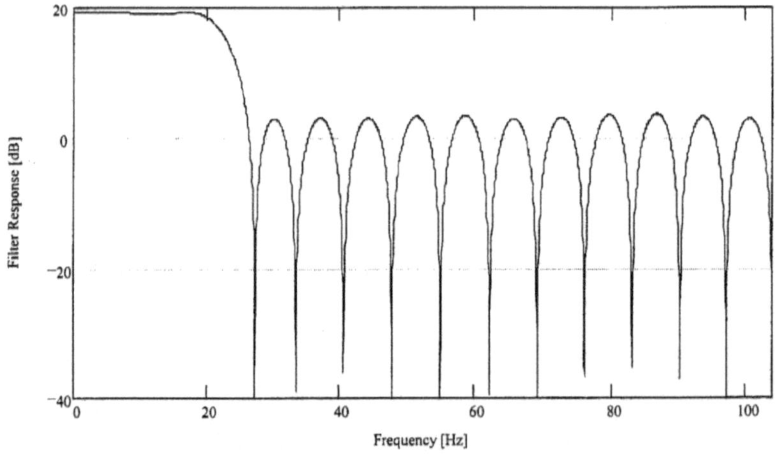

Figure 37: Frequency Response of Filter E

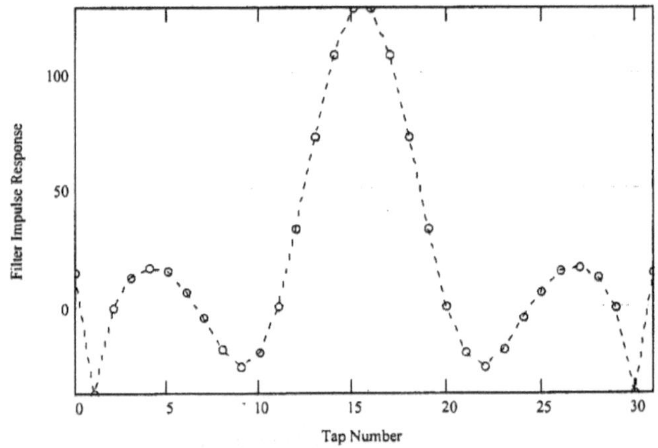

Figure 38: Coefficients of Filter E

A.6 Filter F

This filter was designed using a Linear Method. It was a 32 tap filter designed to operate on data sampled at 208Hz. Its frequency response can be seen in Figure 39 and its filter coefficients in Figure 40

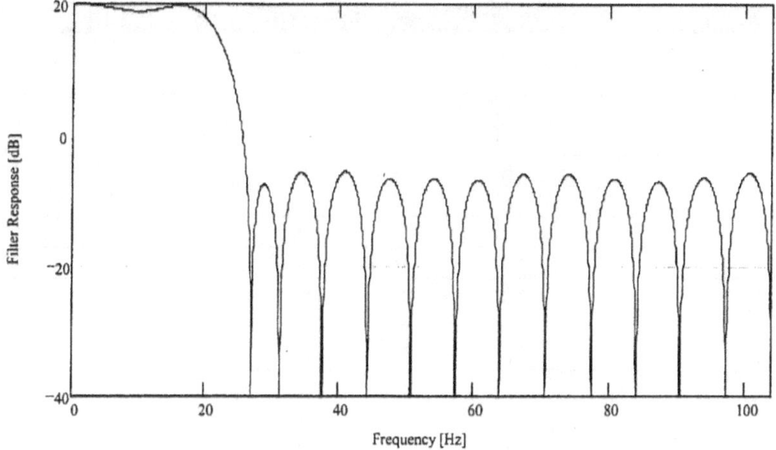

Figure 39: Frequency Response of Filter F

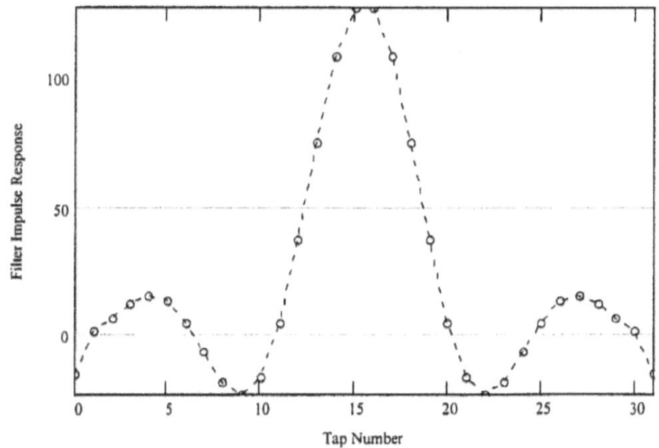

Figure 40: Coefficients of Filter F

A.7   Table of Filter Coefficients

The filter coefficients found in Table 6 were scaled to eight bit, signed integers. These coefficients were used in the testing of the FIR filters described above.

Table 6: FIR Filter Coefficients

Tap Number	Filter A	Filter B	Filter C	Filter D	Filter E	Filter F
1	-3	0	-6	-7	14	-16
2	0	2	-2	-3	-38	1
3	1	2	2	3	-1	6
4	4	0	8	10	12	12
5	6	-1	9	14	16	15
6	8	-3	7	12	15	13
7	10	-3	0	3	6	4
8	12	-2	-10	-9	-5	-7
9	15	0	-19	-21	-19	-19
10	19	3	-20	-25	-26	-24
11	23	5	-13	-18	-20	-17
12	27	4	6	4	0	4
13	32	1	34	37	33	37
14	37	-2	70	75	72	75
15	43	-6	99	108	107	108
16	48	-8	127	127	127	127
17	54	-6	127	127	127	127
18	60	-1	99	108	107	108
19	66	5	70	75	72	75
20	72	11	34	37	33	37
21	78	13	6	4	0	4
22	84	9	-13	-18	-20	-17
23	90	0	-20	-25	-26	-24
24	95	-12	-19	-21	-19	-19
25	100	-22	-10	-9	-5	-7
26	104	-24	0	3	6	4
27	108	-15	7	12	15	13
28	112	6	9	14	16	15
29	114	38	8	10	12	12
30	118	74	2	3	-1	6
31	119	106	-2	-3	-38	1
32	127	127	-6	-7	14	-16
33	127	127				
34	119	106				
35	118	74				
36	114	38				

Tap Number	Filter A	Filter B	Filter C	Filter D	Filter E	Filter F
37	112	6				
38	108	-15				
39	104	-24				
40	100	-22				
41	95	-12				
42	90	0				
43	84	9				
44	78	13				
45	72	11				
46	66	5				
47	60	-1				
48	54	-6				
49	48	-8				
50	43	-6				
51	37	-2				
52	32	1				
53	27	4				
54	23	5				
55	19	3				
56	15	0				
57	12	-2				
58	10	-3				
59	8	-3				
60	6	-1				
61	4	0				
62	1	2				
63	0	2				
64	-3	0				

Appendix B: JTAG Boundary Scan

With the package pin density of many ICs increasing rapidly, conventional methods of testing assembled PCBs are failing to perform adequately. The most common device used for testing assembled PCBs today is the "bed of nails" tester. This device has a number of nail-like probes which are placed on the ICs on the PCB. Different probes are driven by the tester and other probes are then read to see if the correct connection between these test points had been made. The fundamental assumption when using such a tester is that all the pins of the ICs are accessible. This is most certainly not the case with many of the new IC packages e.g. the Ball Grid Array. This is a surface mount device where the "pins" are under the device – inaccessible to any probes.

This problem was recognised and in 1985 and the Joint Test Action Group (JTAG) was formed in an attempt to overcome this problem. Their solution was made an IEEE standard (IEEE 1149.1-1990) and is in use today although it is often still referred to as JTAG. The JTAG solution was to build the test circuitry into the devices, rather than requiring external hardware.

JTAG compliant devices have a 4 pin JTAG port which allows access to the boundary scan hardware. Instructions are loaded into the device in a serial manner while the results are serially read form the device. A number of devices can be connected to the JTAG port in a serial manner. The 4 pin port required on every JTAG port contains two control signals, an input and an output port.

The IEEE Standard IEEE 1149.1-1990 requires that a certain set of instructions be implemented in the boundary scan hardware although the designer is able to able to add support for additional commands [18]. Many of the FPGA manufacturers have extended this port to allow for programming of the devices.

Appendix C: MathCAD SAR Processor

Below is a listing of the MathCAD SAR processor used to test the effects of a presummer and prefilter on SAR processing. The processor generated the returns from a point target which it then presummed and FIR filtered. The presum factor was user definable as was the length of the FIR filter. The coefficients for the filter were read from an ASCII text file. The processed returns were used to construct a matched filter which was then convolved with the processed data. The power values for the focussed image were written to disk where they were analysed by a peak detection program written by Jasper Horrell. The peak width, measured in number of samples, was then input to the processor and the focussed azimuth resolution was then calculated. This was one of the values used to measure the performance of the presummer and FIR filter.

Simple SAR Processor with presummer and filter support

$f_c := 141 \cdot MHz$

Radar carrier frequency

$f_{PRF} := 625 \cdot Hz$

Radar PRF

$$c := 3 \cdot 10^8 \cdot \frac{m}{sec}$$

$$\lambda := \frac{c}{f_c}$$

$\lambda = 2.128 \, m$

$$v := 250 \frac{m}{sec}$$

Speed of aircraft

$\theta_{BW} := 45 \cdot deg$

Antenna beamwidth

$R_t := 6 \cdot km$

Range to target

$Up\_samp := 8$

Upsampling value NB power of 2

$$L_{SA} := \frac{2 \cdot R_t}{\tan\left(\frac{180 \cdot \deg - \theta_{BW}}{2}\right)}$$

$$L_{SA} = 4.971 \cdot km$$

Synthetic Aperture Length

$$dx := \frac{v}{f_{PRF}}$$

$$dx = 0.4$$

Step size

$$Num\_samp := 2^{\operatorname{ceil}\left(\frac{\log\left(\frac{L_{SA}}{dx}\right)}{\log(2)}\right)}$$

$$Num\_samp = 16\vdots$$

Make the array a power of 2 in length

$$R(n) := \sqrt{R_t^2 + \left[\left[\left(n - \frac{Num\_samp}{2}\right) \cdot dx\right]\right]^2} - R_t$$

$$Valid\_samp := \frac{\tan\left(\frac{\theta_{BW}}{2}\right) \cdot R_t}{dx}$$

$$Valid\_samp = 6.2$$

$$i := 0 .. Num\_samp - 1$$

Array index

$$ret_i := 0$$

Clear the contents of the array

$$Valid\_range := \operatorname{ceil}\left(\frac{Num\_samp}{2} - Valid\_samp\right) .. \operatorname{floor}\left(\frac{Num\_samp}{2} + Valid\_samp\right)$$

$$ret_{Valid\_range} := \exp\left(4 \cdot \frac{\pi}{\lambda} \cdot R(Valid\_range) \cdot j\right)$$

Returns from a single target
Doppler BW Calc

$$L_{SA\_Real} := dx \cdot Num\_samp$$

$$L_{SA\_Real} = 6.55\iota$$

$$\operatorname{atan}\left(\frac{L_{SA\_Real}}{2 \cdot R_t}\right) = 28.64$$

Half BW

$$B_D := \frac{4 \cdot v \cdot \sin\left(\operatorname{atan}\left(\frac{2 \cdot dx \cdot Valid\_samp}{2 \cdot R_t}\right)\right)}{\lambda}$$

$$B_D = 179.\iota$$

$$Res := 0.89 \frac{v}{B_D}$$

$$Res = 1.2$$

These write the data to file in an unsigned integer format. Range 0 to 255 with a DC offset of 128. This is used to check the effects of quantisation by allowing the VHDL model to process the data, instead of the MathCAD Simulation

$$\text{WRITEPRN}(\text{DataI}) := 128 + \text{floor}\left(\text{Re}\left(127 \cdot \text{ret}_i\right)\right)$$

$$\text{WRITEPRN}(\text{DataQ}) := 128 + \text{floor}\left(\text{Im}\left(127 \cdot \text{ret}_i\right)\right)$$

First we must presum the return by 3

$$\text{PS\_Fact} := 3$$

$$\text{PSNum\_samp} := \text{floor}\left(\frac{\text{Num\_samp}}{\text{PS\_Fact}}\right)$$

Number of samples after presumming

$$\text{PSNum\_samp} = 546$$

$$a := 0 .. \text{PSNum\_samp} - 1$$

$$\text{PSi} := 0 .. \text{PSNum\_samp} - 1$$

$$\text{ps\_ret}_a := \begin{vmatrix} \text{tmp} \leftarrow 0 \\ \quad \text{for } i \in 0 .. \text{PS\_Fact} - 1 \\ \qquad \text{tmp} \leftarrow \text{tmp} + \text{ret}_{(\text{PS\_Fact} \cdot a + i)} \\ \text{tmp} \end{vmatrix}$$

And now for the FIR filter

$$\text{filter} := \text{READPRN}(t64)$$

$$\text{Filt\_len} := \text{length}(\text{filter})$$

$$\text{Filt\_len} = 64$$

$$\text{left} := \text{ceil}\left(\frac{\text{Filt\_len}}{2}\right)$$

$$\text{left} = 32$$

Finds the midpoint of the filter

$$\text{right} := \text{floor}\left(\frac{\text{Filt\_len}}{2}\right)$$

$$\text{right} = 32$$

$$\text{index} := \text{left} .. \text{PSNum\_samp} - \text{right}$$

$$\text{filt\_ret}_{\text{PSi}} := 0$$

$$\text{filt\_ret}_{\text{index}} := \begin{vmatrix} \text{tmp} \leftarrow 0 \\ \quad \text{for } i \in -(\text{left} - 1) .. \text{right} \\ \qquad \text{tmp} \leftarrow \text{tmp} + \text{filter}_{(\text{left} - 1) + i} \cdot \text{ps\_ret}_{(\text{index} + i) - 1} \\ \dfrac{\text{tmp}}{3} \end{vmatrix}$$

Now we put in a skip factor. This should not be greater than the filter length to avoid data loss

$$\text{Skip\_factor} := 4$$

$$\text{Num\_samp} := 2^{\text{ceil}\left(\dfrac{\log\left(\dfrac{\text{PSNum\_samp}}{\text{Skip\_factor}}\right)}{\log(2)}\right)}$$

$$\text{Num\_samp} = 204$$

New number of samples after presumming and prefiltering

$$j := 0 .. \text{Num\_samp} - 1$$

$$\text{ind} := 0 .. \frac{\text{PSNum\_samp}}{\text{Skip\_factor}} - 1$$

$\text{reduced\_ret}_j := 0$

Setting the new array to zero in case old data is left there

$\text{reduced\_ret}_{ind} := \text{filt\_ret}_{\text{Skip\_factor} \cdot ind}$

$\text{length}(\text{reduced\_ret}) = 2.0$

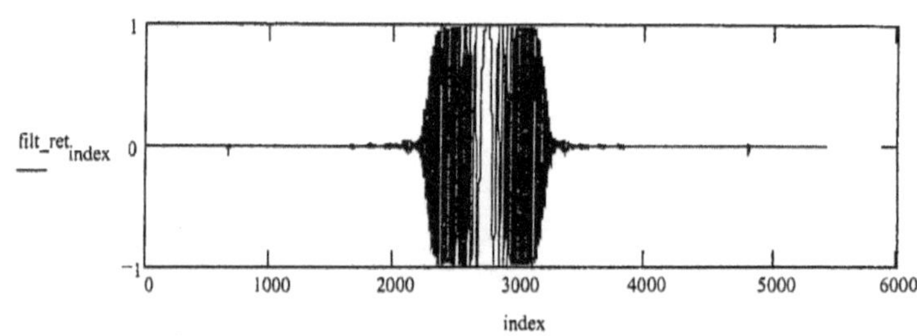

Filtered return shown in
azimuth. Note that the
FIR filter has nulled all
but the center of the
return - that which is
low frequency.

Now calculate the matched filter

$$\text{mf}_j := \overline{\text{reduced\_ret}_{(\text{Num\_samp} - (j+1))}}$$

$\text{length}(\text{mf}) = 2.0$

$k := \text{Num\_samp} .. 2 \cdot \text{Num\_samp} - 1$

$l := 0 .. 2 \cdot \text{Num\_samp} - 1$

Padding for the convolution must be added to avoid wrap around problems

$\text{mf}_k := 0$

$\text{reduced\_ret}_k := 0$

Time for the FFT's!

$\text{freq}_{mf} := \text{cfft}(\text{mf})$

FFT the matched filter

$\text{freq}_{\text{red\_ret}} := \text{cfft}(\text{reduced\_ret})$

FFT the radar return

$\text{freq}_{\text{conv}_l} := \text{freq}_{\text{red\_ret}_l} \cdot \text{freq}_{\text{mf}_l}$

The convolution in the time domain is
equivalent to multiplication in the
frequency domain

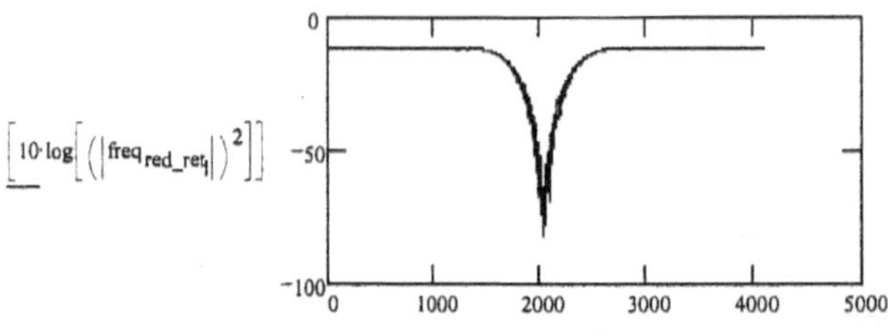

Upsampling time to make prettier images

$$m := 0 .. \left(\frac{\log(\text{Up\_samp})}{\log(2)} \right)$$

$$\text{tst} := \sum_m 2^m - 1$$

$$\text{tst} = 14$$

$$y := \text{Num\_samp} .. \text{Num\_samp} \cdot (\text{tst} + 1) - 1$$

$$n := 0 .. 2 \cdot \text{Up\_samp} \cdot \text{Num\_samp} - 1$$

$$\text{freq conv}_{(\text{tst} \cdot \text{Num\_samp}) + k} := \text{freq conv}_k$$

$$\text{freq conv}_y := 0$$

Now we invert back to the time domain

$$\text{td} := \text{icfft}\left(\text{freq conv} \right)$$

$$o := (\text{Up\_samp} \cdot \text{Num\_samp}) - 100 .. (\text{Up\_samp} \cdot \text{Num\_samp}) + 100$$

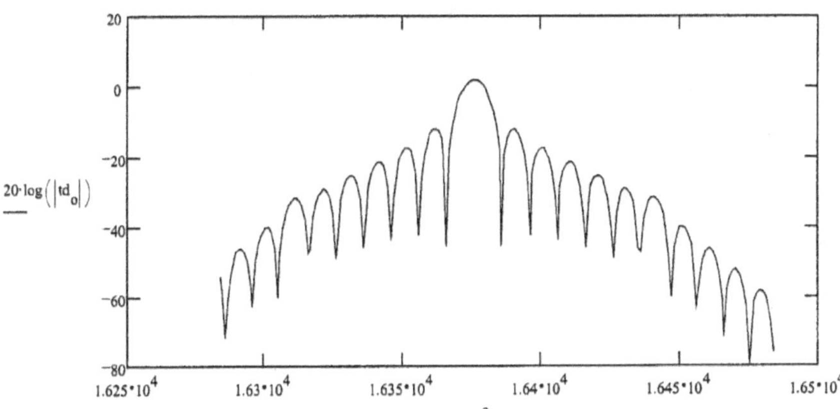

This is a magnified version of the centre section of the image below.

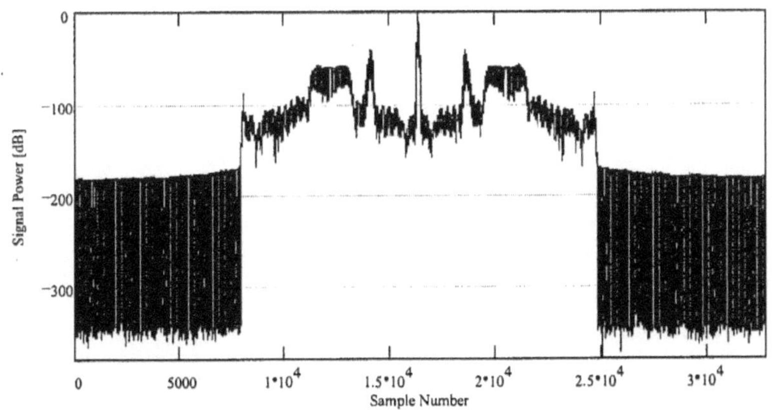

$$\text{WRITEPRN}(\text{focussed}) := \text{Re}\left(\text{td}_o\right)^2 + \text{Im}\left(\text{td}_o\right)^2$$

Write the output power values for processing

$$Real\_res := 8.78 \frac{dx \cdot (Skip\_factor \cdot PS\_Fact)}{Up\_samp}$$

$$Real\_res = 5.268 \, m$$

$$Exp\_res := \frac{v}{40 \cdot Hz} \cdot .89$$

$$Exp\_res = 5.563 \, m$$

$$\frac{Exp\_res - Real\_res}{Exp\_res} = 5.294 \cdot \%$$

Appendix D: VHDL Code Description

This appendix will explain the VHDL code listings found on the enclosed CD-ROM. For the presummer and prefilter there are each three models: the algorithm model, the functional model and the synthesis model. Testbenches for the latter two models are also included as well as some code to create a set of test data. A number of components were written for the presummer and prefilter. These included registers, latches and components that calculated the absolute value of numbers. The testbenches required a RAM model that was written and is also described below.

All of the code used was VHDL '93 compliant and is incompatible with VHDL '87 because of the file handling routines used.

D.1　Test Data Generator

Filename: FILEGEN.VHD

Description: This code creates a set of test data that can be used by the presummer for verification. The program simply loops through the values 0 to 255 for each PRI. A total of 100 PRIs are output, each containing 4096 range bins. This simple, repetitive data was chosen to aid debugging, especially for the prefilter. The output file was in ASCII format it ease debugging.

D.2　RAM Model

Filename: FUNC10BIT.VHD

Description: The data for the RAM structure was taken from [7]. The RAM model stores all the data in a single 128K array of integers. The range of the integers is set to limit the data values to 10 bit precision. Cypress do not produce a 10 bit device but for simulation purposes it was decided to make a 10 bit device instead of using two 8 bit devices. This was done to improve the simulation speed.

The first two processes ("CounterL" and "CounterR") are responsible for handling the address lines. Since the device is dual ported, the two ports are designated as being the left or right port. Separate processes are used for the left and right address signals as they operate off separate clocks. Every time the address strobe is made active, the value on the address bus is latched. If the internal address counter is enabled, this latched address is incremented every clock cycle. The address is reset to zero when the counter is reset.

The "Memory" process performs all the memory reads and writes. This process operates on both the left and right ports as only a single process can drive any one signal. The memory array is declared as a signal. This process is not clocked as all the inputs to it are clocked - hence the process is still synchronous.

The remaining processes ("RegsL" and "RegsR") are used to register the control signals. The remaining code implements multiplexers which are required to make use of extra latches when the RAM is used in pipeline mode.

D.3   Presummer Code

D.3.1   Algorithm Model
Filename: PS_ALG.VHD

Description: This code contains a single process. It has no testbench associated with it as it is the top level simulation. The results need to be verified by hand so that they can be used for testing the less abstract models.

The model makes use of an array of 4096 integers to hold temporary data while the PRIs are being summed. The data values are constrained to the integer equivalent of 10 bits to ensure that there is no overflow.

One process is used to perform all the processing. The input files are first opened and the presum counter is reset. A loop is then used to read in an entire PRI. If the presum counter is zero, the input data is simply stored in the array. If not, it is added to the contents of the array. When the third PRI is summed, the result of each range bin is written to the output file. Once each PRI has been processed, the presum counter is incremented. After three PRIs have been processed, the presum counter is reset.

D.3.2 Functional Model

Filename: PS.VHD

Description: The representation of the data values within the presummer is all integers. This was done to increase the level of abstraction within the model. The advantage of this was the availability of mathematical functions for integer data types.

The first block ("SyncFifoWEn1_n") is used for creating a single pulse which is one clock cycle in length. This is required as the ADCv_n signal is active for more than one clock cycle. Since the FIFO is synchronous, more than one sample would be written if the Write Enable signal was not synchronised.

The next block ("Latches") contains the registers for the inputs and outputs. The adder process that follows it performs the additions which are required for presumming.

The "StateMachine" block has a number of processes that define the state machine behaviour. The states are enumerated and two signals are defined for the current and next states. The state machine encoding style was unimportant in this model as during the functional simulation, no timing constraints were imposed on the model. The first process is used to assign the next state to the current state on each clock cycle. The second process is used to determine the state transitions while the remaining processes use the value of the current state to set their outputs. One process is responsible for the RAM signals, another for the FIFO signals while the last process controls the internal control signals.

D.3.3 Synthesis Model

Filename: PRESUMMER.VHD

Description: This is the code which was used for the synthesis of the presummer.

The first components which were instantiated were the LUTs to remove the DC offset. The I and Q channels each had a dedicated LUT. Both the input and output of the LUTs were registered which meant that the result from the LUT was available after two clock cycles. To ensure that the FIFO data and RAM data were available at the same time, a register was inserted into the RAM data path. This was to hold the RAM data while the LUTs performed their operations on the FIFO data.

The next two blocks ("SyncHBRSel" and "SyncFifoWEn1_n") are used to create a single pulse every time the HBRSel and FIFOWEnl_n signals respectively go active. The pulse generated lasts for one clock cycle. Two flip flops are used in this process.

The "Latches" block contains the instantiations of all the registers. The first two registers are the RAM data registers described above. The RAM address is also registered. The reason for this is to make use of the registers in the I/O blocks of the FPGA. This decreases the clock-to-output time on the address signal. The chip enable signal is also registered.

The "Counters" block contains the instantiations of the counters. As described in Chapter 7: Presummer Design, four counters were required: Two range bin counters ("ColCounterR" and "ColCounterW"), a range line counter ("RowCounter") and a presum counter ("PresumCounter"). The presum counter

The "Adders" block contains the instantiations of the adders. Only a single pipeline stage was used. This was done to decrease the latency of the system as only a single sample would be processed at a time. The adders were 10 bits wide, although the input from the LUTs was 8 bits wide. This input was therefore sign extended to 10 bits.

The "StateMachine" block holds the descriptions of the state machine. One Hot Encoding is used and an index is declared for each state to allow for the enumeration of the states. The first two processes perform the state transitions while the remaining processes in the block are responsible for controlling internal and external signals. Notice should be taken of the "IF" statements used in the output processes. These were used to prevent any comparators from being synthesised. This increased the operating speed of the state machine.

D.3.4 Presummer Testbench

Filename: TB_PS.VHD

Description: The presummer testbench instantiates the presummer and the RAM and connected the two components. The first two processes create the clock signals for the two components. The "Timingcard" process creates the external signals which are input to the presummer (HBRSel and ADCv_n signals).

The "FifoProc" and "FifoReads" processes provide the functionality of the input FIFOs. The first process keeps track of the number of samples which are stored in the FIFO and sets the FIFO empty and full flags accordingly. The second process reads the input data from disk every time a read operation is requested by the presummer. In this way, the sampled data from the ADCs can be simulated.

The "OutputData" process makes use of the right hand port of the dual ported RAM to write the presummed data to disk. Every time the presummer asserts the PSRowDone line to signal that a presummed line has been written to RAM, the process reads another PRI from the RAM which is then written to disk. The process contains counters which operate in the same way as those in the presummer so that the correct RAM addresses can be produced. By making use of the second RAM port, the testbench does not interfere with the operations performed on the RAM by the presummer.

D.4   Prefilter Code

D.4.1 Algorithm Model

Filename: PF_ALG.VHD

Description: This code contains a single process. It has no testbench associated with it as it is the top level simulation. The results need to be verified by hand so that they can be used for testing the less abstract models.

The model makes use of a 2 dimensional array of 4096 x 99 integers to store the data to be prefiltered. A second array of 32 integers contains the coefficients for the FIR filter. The precision of the data is 23 bits while filter coefficients are 8 bits wide.

One process is used to perform all the processing. The input files are first opened and the contents are read into the data array. This model only processes the first 100 PRIs of a data file. The number can be increased by changing the loop variables and dimensions of the data array. A second loop is then used to perform the prefiltering. The result is divided by the correct scale factor and the result is written to disk. A skip factor of four is introduced before the next set of PRIs is processed.

D.4.2 Functional Model
Filename: PF.VHD

Description: The representation of the data values within the prefilter is all integers. This was done to increase the level of abstraction within the model. The advantage of this was the availability of mathematical functions for integer data types.

The "FIRFilter" block implements the FIR filter. An array of 32 integers holds the data to be filtered. On each clock edge, the value on the RAM data bus is clocked into the filter. This data is multiplied by the coefficients and the result is divided by the scale factor.

"PSRowCntProc" is a procedure that implements the presummed row counter. The counter increments when the presummer makes the "PSRowCntInc" line active. When the prefilter makes the "DownCounterEn" line active, then the counter decrements. When both "PSRowCntInc" and "DownCounterEn" and are active, the counter does nothing.

The "StateMachine" block is similar to those descibed in the presummer above. Two processes specify the state transitions while the remaining processes control the outputs and internal control signals.

D.4.3 Synthesis Model

Filename: PREFILTER.VHD

Description: This is the code that was used for synthesising the prefilter. The top level of the design was actually a schematic description so that the FIR filter, written in AHDL, could be linked to the VHDL description of the remaining hardware. The VHDL source code is divided into three main blocks: "PostProcessing", "Counters" and "StateMachine".

The "PostProcessing" block provides all the numerical processing on the data once it has been FIR filtered. Two registers ("FIROutputRegI" and "FIROutputRegQ") are used to latch the correct output from the FIR filter since the filter output is continuous. The state machine controls the register enable signal ("LatchFIRDataEn").

Two absolute value components then process the FIR filter output. These components check the MSB of the incoming data to determine whether the value is positive or negative. Two's complement representation is assumed. If the data is negative, the bits which represent it are inverted and added to 1. If the data is positive, it is merely output. Three pipeline stages were used in the adder. More pipeline stages could have been added if the component was too slow but this was not required.

A pair of dividers is instantiated to divide the absolute value of the FIR filter data. Since this was the slowest part of the circuit, the maximum amount of pipelining was introduced (seven stages). The limit on the number of pipeline stages was specified by the component.

Two pairs of LUTs were required to add the required DC offset – one for positive values and the other for negative values. The outputs of these LUTs were multiplexed so that correct output would be placed on the FIFO data bus. The selection signal for this multiplexer was the MSB of the register that latched the FIR filter output.

The "Counters" block holds all the address and state machine counters. "SampleCounter" and "BinCounter" are the PRI and range bin counters respectively. They are used for generating the RAM address. "StartCounter" contains the start value of the PRI counter which is reloaded after every range bin has been processed. "StartCounter" is only 4 bits wide while "SampleCounter" is 6 bits wide. The reason for this is that "StartCounter" is required to increment in multiples of four. When connected to the PRI counter, the two LSBs are therefore connected to ground.

The width of "BinCounter" is 13 bits instead of the expected 12 bits required to represent 4096 values. The reason for this is that the state machine uses the MSB as the signal to indicate when an entire PRI has been processed. The MSB of the counter is high after 4096 increments. To enable future support for 4096 or 2048 range bins, the two MSBs of the "BinCounter" are connected to a multiplexer. The selection signal ("Bins4096n2048") is used to control the number of range bins per PRI. This signal is pulled high internally as it was not required in this implementation. A simple modification would be required to route this signal to an input pin.

"PSRowCounter" is used to track the number of presummed rows in memory. The "DownCounter" is used to count four clock pulses which will decrement the "PSRowCounter" by four, after each PRI has been processed. The "FIRCounter" is used to count the number of samples that are written into the FIR filter.

The "StateMachine" block is similar to those used in the models above. The first two processes control the state transitions while the remaining processes control the internal and external signals.

The two signals "WriteDataNow" and "LatchDataNow" decode the outputs of "FirCounter" and indicate to the state machine when to latch the FIR filter output data and when to write the processed output to the FIFOs.

D.4.4 Prefilter Testbench
Filename: TB_PF.VHD

Description: The prefilter testbench instantiates the prefilter and the RAM and connects the two components. This testbench operates in the reverse order to the presummer testbench. The data is first written to the RAM through the right hand port from disk. Once the prefilter has filtered the data, it writes it to output FIFOs which are simulated in the testbench. The output data is written to disk.

The "InputData" process is responsible for loading the RAM with the presummed data. One sample is loaded per clock cycle until an entire range line has been loaded. The testbench then waits for the remainder of the PRI and then loads the next range line. After every range line has been written, the testbench asserts the "PSRowCntInc" input for one clock cycle.

The "OutputData" process simulates the behaviour of the output FIFOs. Each time a write operation is requested, the testbench writes the data on the FIFO data bus to disk.

REFERENCES

1. Altera, FIR Filters, Functional Specification 1, Version 1, Altera Corporation, 1996.

2. Altera, Implementing FIR Filters in FLEX Devices, Application Note 73, Version 1.01, Altera Corporation, 1998.

3. Altera, State Machine Encoding, Application Brief No. 131, Altera Corporation, 1994.

4. Anderson A.H., Downs G.S., Shaw G.A., RASSP Benchmark –1 and –2: Preliminary Assessment, 2nd RASSP Conference http://rassp.aticorp.org/public/confs/2nd/anderson.pdf, 1995

5. Andraka R., Multiplication in FPGAs, http://users.ids.net/~randraka/multipli.htm, 1998.

6. Baluja S., Population-Based Incremental Learning: A Method for Integrating Genetic Search Based Function Optimisation and Competitive Learning, http://www.cs.cmu.edu/afs/cs/user/baluja/www/papers/CMU-CS-94-163.ps.gz, 2 June 1994.

7. Cypress, CY7C09099 Data Sheet, http://www.cypress.com, 1997.

8. Habinc S., VHDL Models for Board-level Simulation, *IEEE Design and Test of Computers*, Fall 1996, pp 66-78.

9. Harris F.J., On the use of windows for harmonic analysis with the Discrete Fourier Transform, *IEEE Proceedings*, vol. 66, no. 8, 1 January 1978, pp. 51-83.

10. Myers C., Fiore P., Letellier J.P., Rapid Development of Signal Processors and the RASSP Program, IEEE International Workshop in Rapid System

Prototyping, http://rassp.aticorp.org/public/sanders/rassp-program.pdf, June 1994.

11.   Navabi Z., VHDL Analysis and Modelling of Digital Systems, Second Edition, McGraw-Hill, 1998.

12.   Oppenheim A.V., Schafer R.W., Discrete-Time Signal Processing, Prentice-Hall International Inc., 1989.

13.   Pridmore J.S., Schaming W.B., RASSP Methodology Overview, 1st RASSP Conference, http://rassp.scra.org/public/confs/1st/PRIDMORE94A.PDF, 1994.

14.   RASSP Taxonomy Working Group, RASSP VHDL Modelling Terminology and Taxonomy, http://www.atl.external.lmco.com/rassp/taxon/rassp_taxon.html, June 1998.

15.   Richards M.A., The Rapid Prototyping of Application Specific Signal Processors (RASSP) Program: Overview and Status, 1st RASSP Conference, http://rassp.scra.org/public/confs/1st/rassp-overview.pdf, 1994.

16.   Selesnick I.W., Lang M., Barrus C.S., Constrained Least Square Design of FIR Filters Without Specified Transition Bands, *IEEE Trans. on Signal Processing*, vol. 44, no. 8, August 1996, pp. 1879-1892.

17.   Shaw G.A., RASSP Benchmark Program Overview, 1st RASSP Conference, http://rassp.scra.org/public/confs/1st/bmoverview.pdf, 1994.

18.   Texas Instruments, IEEE Std 1149.1-1990 (JTAG) Testability, http://www.ti.com/sc/docs/jtag/jtaghome.htm, 1997.

19.   Tréméac Y., Inggs M.R., An example of rapid prototyping on the TMS320C80 multimedia video processor (MVP), Proceedings of the South African Symposium on Communications and Signal Processing, September 1998, pp 233-237.

20.   Xilinx, The Programmable Logic Data Book, Xilinx Inc., 1998.

BIBLIOGRAPHY

- Drieling R., Processes and Experiences in VHDL Top Down Design, http://rassp.scra.org/public/sanders/vhdl-top-down-design.pdf.

- Fiore P.D., Will E., Edelson G., Herold D., Rapid Prototyping Applied to Underwater Acoustic Model Research and Development, http://rassp.scra.org/public/confs/2nd/FIORE95A.PDF, 1995

- Gradient A.J., Madisetti V.K., Aylor J.H., Wilsey D.P., A Paradigm Shift in Digital System Design Education with Industry Participation, Proceedings of the American Society for Engineering Education, http://rassp.scra.org/public/ef/asee_fin.pdf, June 1996

- Habinc S., VHDL Models for Board-level Simulation, http://rassp.aticorp.org/vhdl/guidelines/BoardLevel.ps.gz, February 1996.

- Hein C., Nasoff D., VHDL-Based Performance Modelling and Virtual Prototyping, http://rassp.aticorp.org/public/confs/2nd/HEIN95B.PDF, 1994

- Hein C., Pridgen J., Kline W., RASSP Virtual Prototyping of DSP Systems, http://www.sigda.acm.org/Dac/34dac/papers/1997/dac97/pdffiles/30_2.pdf, 1997.

- Hood B., Viewpoint from a Prime Developer, http://rassp.scra.org/public/sanders/rassp-viewpoint.pdf, Lockheed Sanders.

- Johnson D., Keeping Your Programmable Logic Design On Track, http://www.appreview.com/AppSearch/Pdf/CYPRESS1997Q4.PDF, 3 November 1997.

- Linderman R., VHDL for the Schematic Designer, http://www.appreview.com/AppSearch/Pdf/SYNARIO1997Q4.PDF, 3 November 1997.

- Naval Surface Warfare Center, Naval Air Warfare Center (Aircraft Division), Naval Research Laboratory, A VHDL Modelling Guide, ftp://130.163.68.110/Tirep/Guide/vhdlmg20.zip, 31 January 1995.

- Powell S.R., Cesear T.M., Rapid Design and Exploration of Signal Processing Systems using a VHDL Model Generator Based Paradigm, http://rassp.aticorp.org/public/confs/2nd/dqdt.pdf, 22 August 1995.

- Pridgen J., Jaffe R., Kline W., RASSP Technology Insertion into the Synthetic Aperture Radar Image Processor Application, http://rassp.scra.org/public/atl/pridgen.pdf.

- Pridmore J., Advanced Technology Laboratories' Path to 4X Improvements, http://rassp.scra.org/public/atl/pridmore.pdf, Lockheed Sanders.

- Scanlan L., Rapid Prototyping of Application-specific Signal Processors (RASSP), http://rassp.scra.org/public/sanders/scanlan-rassp.pdf.

- Shaw G.A., Zuerndorfer B.W., Ford R.A., Anderson J.C., Anderson A.H., RASSP Benchmark 2 Technical Description, http://llex.ll.mit.edu/llrassp/bm2.ps.Z, 10 August 1995.

- Sinander P., The Usage of VHDL in the European Space Agency, ftp://ftp.estec.esa.nl/pub/vhdl/doc/UseOfVHDL.ps, 1995.

- Sinander P., VHDL Modelling Guidelines, http://rassp.aticorp.org/vhdl/guidelines/ModelGuide.ps.gz, September 1994.

- Zuerndorfer B., Anderson J.C., Ford R.A., Anderson A.H., Rocco G.A., Shaw G.A., RASSP Benchmark 1 Technical Description, http://llex.ll.mit.edu/llrassp/bm1.ps.Z, 13 December 1994.

- Zuerndorfer B., Shaw G A, SAR Processing for RASSP Application http://llex.ll.mit.edu/llrassp/bwz/rasspcon3.ps.Z.